LAST TRAIN TO MACHU PICCHU

LAST TRAIN TO MACHU PICCHU

A Memoir of a Medical Mission Worker in an Indigenous Village High in the Andes Mountains of Peru

HANNAH HANNON

Book Design & Production:
Columbus Publishing Lab
www.ColumbusPublishingLab.com

Copyright © 2025 by
Hannah Hannon
LCCN: 2025909089

All rights reserved.
This book, or parts thereof, may not be
reproduced in any form without permission.

Paperback ISBN: 978-1-63337-933-6
E-Book ISBN: 978-1-63337-935-0

Printed in the United States of America
1 3 5 7 9 10 8 6 4 2

Cover art "Lake Titicaca"
by Hannah Hannon

To my family, my heart, my joy.
Trish & Rod, Jack & Jane

"And when you turn to the right or when you turn to the left, your ears shall hear a word behind you saying, 'This is the way; walk in it.'" —Isaiah 30:21

Introduction

I'VE BEEN reluctant at times to say I believe in God, especially when that belief has seemed distorted into a political movement of a different spirit than mine. In public, I've sometimes hid my Peru crucifix under my shirt.

When I first started writing about my experience as a medical missioner in an indigenous village in the Andes, one writer asked me, "What is the arc of your story?" I had no idea.

But now, having written it, having lived twenty years past those years in Peru, I do know.

The underlying arc of my story, along with sharing the experience of living in an indigenous mountain village for three years, is how I found my way to becoming my authentic self. This process for me is about getting close to God and making it a vital priority to figure out who God made me to be.

I realize I know very little about God. Some call God the Ground of All Being, or Love, or the Creator of All. I believe that all of these are aspects of God, but I also believe that God is a being, with a personhood.

As Father Richard Rohr, the founder of the Center for Action and Contemplation in New Mexico, asserts, "God wants a relationship with us." That has been a priceless learning. It has strengthened my acceptance of feeling guided by God.

I've read Father Rohr's books and been gifted by his daily website for decades, in the morning sun on a primitive porch in Peru, or in more conventional settings wherever I've lived. He grew me up in my religion.

"It doesn't get any better than that," as he would say.

This book is mostly about my three years with Maryknoll Missions in the high Andes. I wanted my kids to know what I was doing during the years I was out of the country. They were married and making good lives when I left. They still are, now with me a part of it. I am happy to my core to be back with all of them. This is the story of my Peru experience, arc and all.

Chapter 1
Night Call

IT'S COLD at 13,000 feet. I'm under layers of heavy blankets, Peru style. I wake for a moment with the effort of turning over under the weight, just as a loud knock jolts me upright. My heart pounds. Someone has trespassed through our gate into the yard, right to my bedroom door! This is not done here!

I'm relieved to hear young female voices calling out.

"*Hermana!* Sister!" they call. To the Aymara people, all marriage-aged women living alone must be nuns.

"Sister, our brother is hurt, can you come?!"

I hesitate. I've been trying to promote regular clinic hours, preferably starting after my morning coffee. But the Aymara people keep to their own rhythms. It's barely dawn when they typically knock at my outside gate. They've been gathering fodder for their animals from nearby Lake Titicaca. If I miss seeing them then, I miss them for the day, as they need to go on from there to tend their fields.

But this is what I came for, why I made a three-year commitment to Maryknoll Missions after a year of training and language school with them.

"Okay, let me get dressed," I say.

We start climbing up the hill. I need a flashlight; the girls don't seem to. Village dogs bark in the distance. It's chilly, but the climbing is keeping me warm. I finger bread I have in my pocket to lure the dogs away from us if they come too close. I have a few rocks too, to scare off the dogs if needed. With a little more walking, we arrive. I shrug off my bag, a little breathless from the climb.

The girls call out to announce us. Their home is typical, three small adobe buildings with thatched roofs. I enter behind them into one room that I see is the family bedroom. It contains sturdy pine beds and heavy clothing hung on hooks. The electricity is working; there's a single bulb in the ceiling. I can see sufficiently.

The hurt brother is sitting up, damp hair hanging over his flushed face. A young woman sits in a chair by his bed, her head down, eyes on her tightly folded hands. In the far corner, two *anciaños*, old folks, are huddled together in a bed wearing wool hats and shawls. The third bed belongs to the girls. They had told me he couldn't walk. It dawns on me to ask how he got home. "We helped him," they say in unison, perhaps having rehearsed their answer. I smile.

The patient, Antonio, tells me what happened. He'd been drinking and got into a fight at a wedding. I've never seen the people in my village drink alcohol except at weddings and festivals.

Antonio says he's not peeing blood, and I check that he doesn't have a temperature or broken bones. I moisten a cloth in bottled water and wash his face. I see he is more shaken up than physically injured. I dig out a bottle of valerian root from my bag and give him a spoonful and some ibuprofen. I wrap two more pills in paper from my notepad.

"Take these in the morning with breakfast. You'll be all right," I reassure him. "Come see me if anything gets worse."

Night Call

He seems relieved and ready for sleep. So does his young wife.

As I pack up my bag, the grandmother signals my attention and points to her husband's leg. I peer down, aiming my flashlight. His thin lower leg is mottled with small red mounds that look like unhealed diabetic sores.

"How long has he had these?" I ask. The girls translate my Spanish into Aymara.

The young usually have Spanish, but not the old folks. "*Años*," they translate the old woman saying. "Years." "For this one," I say, "come to the clinic tomorrow."

The sun is just breaking through as I walk back down, lighting up the smoky mist hovering over the fields. I'm glad to see my own collection of rooms. Glad to see the sign in my clinic window, *Clinica de Las Cordilleras*, Clinic of the High Mountains. And no one is waiting at the gate.

Chapter 2
Why'd You Go to Peru?

DRIVING ALONG Lake Titicaca, I glance at the long reeds fanned out on the grassy banks. The villagers pull out the shoots to dry, using them to weave thatched roofs. Red-tipped quinoa sways slightly as I pass, soon ready for harvest. I love the smell of fresh-turned dirt, dark as chocolate. There are few trees at this altitude. It can look and feel desolate, but not today.

I'm on my way to the pharmacy to pick up supplies for a clinic I share with Suzanne, the nurse practitioner here for years with her husband and young son. On the way, I'll pick up my mission partner, Lexi.

Maryknoll sends each year's class out two by two. We've been here about a month. Lexi's a forty-something woman from Manhattan. She's fun, assertive, kind, and mischievous. She sneaks us out of boring meetings, curses imaginatively when frustrated, and helps me faithfully.

I have the Land Rover today. Lexi and I share it, renting it from Father Bob, a Maryknoll priest. The old Land Rover, faded red, came with a large rock and a big nail to whack the battery into life when needed.

I was always drawn to Maryknoll. I'd read their magazine as I rode the trolley to high school, imagining myself living the exotic life of a medical missioner. But around that time, I met a more compelling dream, a fun, good-looking soccer player. Even after dating him, I went off to college on scholarship to Carnegie Tech as a drama major, inspired by starring in high school plays. But when no scholarship was confirmed for the next years, and my family was not able to afford tuition, I came back home after one enriching year of being in lots of plays and living on my own. It was a kind of finishing school I thought when I looked back. I got a job working at the United Airlines ticket counter at the Philadelphia airport and dated the soccer player, Jack Hannon. We married and had two wonderful little redheads, Trish and Jack.

I was on my own again by age thirty. We were too young, I think, to maintain all a marriage calls for. But we kept a healthy, sane relationship after we parted. Jack was a wonderful, involved father, taking the kids sailing, and teaching them the love of sports and how to have fun. He was a full-fledged papa. (Poppa, my kids call him.)

As a single mom, I worked in a newspaper composing room and took college classes, finally graduating to a job at a community mental health clinic. Working there, I earned a master's degree in clinical social work and spent the years the kids were growing up working happily as a therapist.

When my kids were living on their own, I started going on Maryknoll's short-term mission trips to Mexico and Guatemala. Because I'd enjoyed taking Spanish classes, I chose these countries. During my last trip to El Paso, Texas, and across the border to Juarez, I got serious about going ahead with my dream of a three-year commitment to an overseas mission site with Maryknoll.

I lived on my own in a lovely old New Jersey town, where I'd often take walks along the nearby Delaware River. One autumn

Why'd You Go to Peru?

Saturday, off from work, I was luxuriating in my home, a little fire crackling in the wood stove. I was in a kind of reverie, and it felt like other women were in the room with me, each presenting arguments for or against my signing on with Maryknoll. In reality, the women were parts of me, come alive in my imagination.

There was the Frank Lloyd Wright connoisseur, impeccably dressed in camel wool slacks, a silk blouse, and tasteful (i.e. expensive) shoes, insisting I spend my life perfecting my house.

"Fill it with American Craft furniture," she said, "Imagine Tiffany lamps and other lovely things slowly and pleasurably acquired over time."

That'd be a lovely life, I remember thinking. *I have good friends here, other single women.*

We often go into Philadelphia to the art cinema and for dinner. It would be nice.

The spunky adolescent, more freewheeling, given to blaring rock music while driving fast on backroads, not unacquainted with marijuana, spoke up,

"Are you crazy? Give up all this you've spent your adult life earning? Its wonderful here! You have a luxurious life - just enjoy it!"

A young woman in jeans spoke up. "Do something worthwhile, something that helps people. You would love living in another country for three years. You would feel good about yourself. You could really learn Spanish and have a whole new life experience."

By my June birthday that year, I had clarity. I did love my house and the prospect of having beautiful clothes, but I knew that could end up being repetitive and empty.

I loved the spirited freewheeling teenager, but being driven by passion felt unstable. I loved to have fun, but didn't want "SHE WAS A POTHEAD" on my tombstone.

I knew how I'd feel being useful; my core was drawn toward altruism and developing a strong spirit. And I wanted a new life experience. I was drawn to the unknown of an adventure.

The dream for me always included medical training. Training as a physician assistant, a PA, a two-year intensive medical training, was the realistic choice at that point. I planned to apply to PA school, then work in a medical practice to get my sea legs, then apply to Maryknoll.

Now, rolling along to pick up Lexi, I'm living it. She sees me coming and waves from where she's waiting on the highway.

"Did the car start without the rock and nail?"

· · · · ·

We're laughing and looking forward to showers and a washing machine at Maryknoll's Center House in Puno, our nearest town. Lots of missioners from Maryknoll and other organizations come to the Center House, so there's always good company. There's a TV (news in Spanish, of course) and a library, a fireplace and a beautiful chapel. Above all, there are several computers, the lifeline to my family.

Chapter 3
Hope is Where Your Feet Go

YEARS AGO, I read a saying by Daniel Berrigan, a Catholic priest and fierce anti-war activist. "Hope is where your feet go."

Now, soon ready to apply to Hahnemann University, over the bridge in Philadelphia for physician assistant training, I am excited to be actually moving my feet toward learning medicine and then going to foreign mission with Maryknoll.

I finished two prerequisite biology courses at my local community college and decided to start volunteering at a health clinic in Camden, New Jersey, a poor neighborhood only twenty minutes away. I begin working there one morning a week when I have evening hours on my counseling job. But I soon hit a snag.

All the staff are supportive and helpful, except one, a physician assistant, and ironically, a nun. "The mean nun," I call her when I tell my friends about her. The nun seems to purposely ignore me, never offering any teaching. One day she tells me her nephew is also applying to Hahnemann's PA program, then she adds, her face devoid of expression, "I put in a good word for him. I didn't mention you."

I do my best to shed my hurt feelings and soldier on, but at one point the nun says, "I can't trust your blood pressures."

That panicked me. I plan to put the Camden Clinic experience on my application. I can't tell Hahnemann I was fired as a volunteer.

I go to my nurse friend Judy. She and her daughter-in-law, Rowena, give me a hands-on tutorial one Saturday morning in an empty room at their hospital. When I go back to the clinic, I tell the mean nun that a nurse friend has given me good training in taking blood pressures. "You don't have to worry about mine anymore."

Not long after, I ask my friend Dolores to drive with me to Center City Philadelphia to pick up an application for Hahnemann. Dolores disparages the idea. "You have a great job as a therapist; you're finally off beeper duty!"

Dolores has known me for years, including back when I was a social worker in a hospital - based mental health emergency service with varied hours. I'd sometimes be on home-call, my kids knowing to answer the phone "Emergency Service" if they picked up. Their friends were used to the strange greeting. Then I'd go to a quiet room to talk with a patient or his or her family.

Sometimes on call meant going out to a site for a commitment screening. One winter night, I was called to a police station. On the way I managed to lock my keys in the car while parked by a phone booth to make a call for directions.

It was dark and wet and cold, my two kids, teenagers at the time, were home alone asleep. Somehow a cop came along and got my car open. I drove on to Gloucester, the mean streets of Gloucester I called it, especially that night as I drove through the sinister feeling town with wet, slick streets. The officer on duty led me to a cell where a naked guy was lying on the cell floor, babbling under a mattress. I did the commitment process.

My friend Dolores has a point. It is wonderful to have finally graduated (after about eight years of part-time undergraduate classes, then graduate school) and now seeing patients during the day in a nice, sunny office.

"Maybe I'm bored."

"So be bored," she says. She of the lasting marriage, four children, having published a book of her bread recipes. But it isn't boredom. I want to have a different experience. I'm not going to be a doctor at this point in my life, but I can be a PA and a lay missioner.

Always a good friend, Dolores drives me over the bridge to Philadelphia, where we soon are negotiating traffic on Broad Street. We find Hahnemann and the right office and pick up the application.

A few days later, I return alone to drop off the filled-out papers. As I leave, driving past the building, I see a dark-haired woman in a lab coat leaning against the wall, one leg bent back with her foot on the wall for balance. As I glance at the doctor to be, she pushes off the wall, starting toward the curb with a confidence and grace that mesmerizes me.

That, I think, *is who I want to be.*

Chapter 4
Guided

AFTER SUBMITTING the application, I slip back into routine. It's an easy drive back and forth to the counseling center to see my patients, afterward sitting comfortably on my back deck, sipping a glass of iced white wine among my tropical plants in their colorful Mexican pots.

Some Sundays I drive to visit my parents at their nursing home. I find them on the patio contentedly throwing breadcrumbs to the birds. My sister and I have worked out an every-other- Sunday schedule.

But after a few months, I'm worrying. The physician assistant program starts in August, just a couple of months away. I haven't heard from Hahnemann except for the notification that they received my application. Being trained as a PA is a vital step for me in doing overseas mission. I want a practical focus where I'm stationed, and I've wanted medical training for a long time.

So that week at work I'm preoccupied as I get up from my desk to walk to the office of our psychiatrist, Dr. Roth, to consult him about one of my patients. While he's checking the patient's medications, I glance up to see a degree from Hahnemann on his wall.

The question pops out of my mouth.

"Will you write me a letter of recommendation to Hahnemann?" "Sure."

Back in my office, I call the PA program, "May I bring in a letter of recommendation to add to my application file?"

The next morning, on one of my 1 to 9 p.m. days, I drive to Hahnemann with the letter. In the corridor on the way to Admissions, I recognize the name of one of the teachers from the PA brochure. Glad I'm in work clothes, I knock.

"I'm just going to add a letter of recommendation to my file," I say, "and thought I'd introduce myself and meet you."

She's gracious and encouraging. "That's a good idea," she says, and asks me about my work.

Two weeks later I get a phone call telling me I'm accepted. I cry on the phone with the Admissions person, the one who had previously guided me to the exact classes I needed to take at community college to fulfill Hahnemann's prerequisites. On my last day volunteering at the Camden Clinic, one of the young nurses whispers to me that the mean nun's nephew was not accepted.

Chapter 5
PA School

ONE EVENING, I come home tired from work, it's late summer, just weeks before starting PA school. As I plod through the side yard gate, I'm startled to see the patch of ground cover under my pretty cherry tree is now all sand, carved in curved swirls, like a Zen Garden.

It's unexpected. I wasn't consulted.

I call my son, who mows my lawn. He created it as a surprise, he tells me, thinking I'd love it. He and his wife Jane live within walking distance.

I try to mellow out, reminding myself of his always willing help and remembering a previous surprise last winter. I came home to see Christmas tree lights twinkling in my windows. Jack and Jane had set up and decorated my tree.

And when I was planning to move from my previous home, he helped get it ready for sale by digging out several overgrown evergreen bushes, all trunks and dead foliage, right in front. Then he painted the house!

Soothed, I head for my Mexican pots on the back porch, juggling an iced glass of white wine and a library murder mystery.

My son! *Mi hijo*, I call him, and he calls me Mamacita, both of us Spanish students. One time when he was in high school, he stood emptying my grocery bag at the kitchen counter, calling out the items as he dug them out, Ah! *huevos!* (eggs) *leche!* (milk) *dulces!* (cookies). His comic timing could always make Trish and me laugh.

As I drive back and forth the last few days before ending my job, it helps to play Richard Rohr's Enneagram cassettes. A nun, Sister Donna, who lives in the next town from me in New Jersey, gifted me with the set of tapes, starting my lifelong appreciation of Father Richard who I consider my spiritual guide. Ironically, I met Donna in Antigua, Guatemala, and would likely never have met her locally. The Enneagram, an early personality system, is fascinating to work through and identify yourself without question. I remember Trish and I laughing at a cartoon version of a very emotional Type Four, (me) sobbing at her desk in her office.

Finally in that summer of routine, it's time to start PA school. That first day we are scheduled for individual interviews. I enter the office and sit before a relaxed, ginger-haired professor. She smiles up at me. We chat casually, then she mentions that I had a lot of various jobs: newspaper copy editor, substitute teacher, mental health emergency worker, and therapist.

"Which was your favorite job?" she asks.

I told myself in preparing for the interview that I'd just be honest, so I say the simple truth, "Raising my two kids."

She smiles like she understands, and says, "I have kids, I get it."

Next on the agenda is a reception, mingling this year's new PA students and the second- year students. Certification as a physician assistant takes two years. A second-year student at the welcoming gathering tells me, "It's grueling, but if this is what you want, you'll love it."

PA School

As I head to the next event, I'm reacting with a spike of anxiety to a handout showing a lecture scheduled every morning starting at 8 a.m. with tests every Friday.

In the large auditorium, we're told this will be our main classroom for the first year. We're asked to stand up and say why we are choosing to be trained as a PA. I say, "I'm planning to do mission work in Guatemala."

I loved my time in Antigua, Guatemala, with its green rolling hills, and warm people. I lived with a family. If we'd bump into each other a few blocks from their house, the mother would say, "*¡Qué Milagro!*" What a miracle! It was my longest mission to date, almost two months.

One day there I sought a breezy refuge outside my bedroom on a little patch of flat roof. The mother let me know that this was "*prohibido*." The next day on my walk up our street to language school, I saw armed soldiers about every four feet. The President of Guatemala had been staying just across the way that weekend.

Most days there I worked at an orphanage, reading to the kids, just engaging them, helping wherever I could. One likable kid absconded with one of the books I had brought.

I made a deal.

"If you return the book, I'll give it to you to keep when I leave." He did and I did.

As I begin the year, I do love PA school, and it is grueling. During the first few weeks of school I take the light rail train just down my street, switching to the El train in Camden that takes me to Philadelphia. I soon discover this takes too much time. I find a five dollar a day parking lot and drive in every day, playing study cassette tapes in the car. No more Richard Rohr psychology tapes.

I envy the kids who gain study time by just walking to their dorm a block away, and I envy their fun and camaraderie. Out of our class of one hundred I am among a handful of students over age fifty.

Hahnemann assigns us to study medical terminology a few months before starting. That helps a lot, but I have many gaps in my knowledge. As I start classes, I learn others have been nurses or emergency med techs or phlebotomists. One fellow student is telling me a story and I have to ask, "What does *status/post* surgery mean? I soon learn that it's the patient's status after (post)/surgery.

PA school's two years are like medical school compressed; I tell my friends. Morning lectures every day: anatomy, systems of the body, pharmacology. One late-afternoon class at the end of the day; there's usually a fan whirring rhythmically in that room. I have to fight sleep.

We have hands-on labs. We are learning how to give needles by sliding them into oranges. We learn how to suture practicing on chicken breasts, and how to apply casts by encasing each other. We administer and read EKGs, we test nerves, reflexes, and heart sounds. We learn the signs and symptoms of common and uncommon presenting problems, always being trained to ask ourselves, "Is there anything life- threatening here?"

By the second month, I'm taking the histories of real patients in the adjoining hospital, all to be written up in great detail, running ten to twelves pages. I'm studying every evening and all day on the weekends, often getting up to study when my brain is fresh at 4:00 a.m.

Early in the year, when I am still using public transportation, I slump into a seat on the El at the end of the day, then realize with a shock that I have that afternoon class! I get off at the next stop and take a returning El and just make it to class, definitely not falling asleep that day.

Exhausted from getting up so early and overwhelmed by the amount and depth of material I need to master, I feel in over my head. I go to see my friend Judy and spill out my fears.

Judy, a devout Christian, hears me out. We're sitting in her living room. Her house is an A- frame, filled with soft afternoon light playing on her pastel-colored walls.

"I'm serious," I say,"I'm not just looking for sympathy. I'm starting to make the assessment that I'm just not smart enough to do this."

She gives me a look and asks, "Do you think God is a trickster?" "No!"

"Do you think God would give you the inspiration to do this, make it happen, then pull the rug out, saying ha-ha?"

I'm stunned. Judy's right and I know it. Driving home, I pray my thanks. I need to take each next step, give it my honest best.

The second year is a series of rotations. We are scheduled to work five weeks each in psychiatry, cardiology, obstetrics, surgery, pediatrics, and the ER at various hospitals or outpatient clinics. If we don't get a passing grade from the doctor on the rotation site, the rotation has to be repeated.

In the first year of nonstop study and testing, another PA student, Johanna, has become a friend. We occasionally go to a quiet coffee shop around the corner from school that has mismatched old furniture and a sleepy cat on a nearby windowsill. She and I enjoy the rare free time together.

One day when we are talking about a class, she says casually, "We don't do it that way at our clinic."

I say, "What do you mean, your clinic? You're a student like me."

She explains that she and her partner Mary Beth founded an inner-city Catholic Worker Free Health Clinic years ago and she works there on a regular basis.

Because of my more than twenty years as a therapist, I am given permission to do my first rotation, psychiatry, at their clinic. This is a huge blessing. It gives me a chance to get used to the role of being a medical provider, meeting expectations in an unfamiliar field of knowledge.

Heading for the first day of my five-week rotation at my friend's clinic, I am maneuvering my car under the grungy elevated train tracks. *This looks like a set out of West Side Story*, I think. I am lost too, not uncommon for me.

I go into a little store under the El to ask directions and wait behind a large woman dressed in a black leather jacket wearing a neckband with large, protruding silver spikes. I can't help looking at her.

"What are you looking at?" she asks me fiercely. "The cigarettes. I'm looking at the cigarettes."

Ever after, my adult kids love to laugh about Mom and "Betty Big Boots."

The volunteer nurses and doctors at the inner-city clinic help me increase my rudimentary knowledge and boost my confidence for the next five rotations. One nurse sees me struggling with the disposable covering on a thermometer, not able to get it off.

"Oh, those are always tricky to get off," she says, showing me.

Later looking back, it helps me remember to be kind to students fumbling with seemingly simple materials.

My next three rotations are in a large Philadelphia hospital, cardiology, surgery and obstetrics. The hours are long and unpredictable, including time in the operating room.

In the OR, I am invited to close a simple incision. Mostly OR is hours of standing by the operating table, stiff with the effort of trying not to contaminate the sterile field by getting too close to the table. I'm sent on an errand one day to the administrative offices across the street, and I relish the sun on my face for the first time in weeks.

At times, assigned to the night shift, students are permitted to sleep in one of the sleeping rooms for residents. The first time, dead on my feet, I ask a nurse at the nurse' station if she knows where the resident's sleeping room is. "No," is all she answers, her face set. I find it eventually on my own, a little closet with a recliner.

During the hospital rotation, we have lockers. I'm fumbling to open mine one day and drop my combination lock on the floor, which is ankle deep with crumpled paper and discarded socks and face masks.

"I hate this so much," I moan as I grapple through the rubble for my lock.

My pediatric rotation is in a doctor's practice in a Northeast Philadelphia community that serves Russian immigrants. It's a challenge to keep the complicated pediatric immunization schedule straight and learn how to properly diagnose real kids. PAs are never the sole provider at this stage. Doctors are good about answering questions and showing the way. I have an affirming moment during this rotation when I'm examining a thin little boy, newly immigrated from Russia. I'm listening to his heart and lungs. I listen closely again and call the doctor to listen.

"Good catch," he says.

The boy's heart sounds are on the wrong side. It is called transposition of the great vessels, and it needs lifelong awareness and special care. I learn to appreciate paying close attention doing routine exams.

The ER rotation is hard. Being single and not having little kids at home as some of my fellow students do, I am assigned to an out-of-town location, Bridgeport, Connecticut. I'm in a nurses' dorm. I walk to my rotating shifts through a dim, echoing tunnel under the hospital.

Sometimes we have a lecture in the middle of the night, for example, how to treat a rape victim and administer the rape kit at 3am.

As a saving grace, I am able to visit my friend Sheila, funny and warm-hearted; she's an old soul, I always tell her. She lives not far from the hospital in a little cottage by Long Island Sound. She makes me a delicious home-cooked dinner, which we eat on her sun-filled enclosed porch overlooking the water. Sheer bliss.

Mostly, ER is long hours. When an obvious psychiatric case comes in one night, I am drawn to the man and feel able to do a useful evaluation. My suggestion is dismissed by the doctor in charge. In the ER setting, people are very sick and sometimes in severe pain. I do a lot of shadowing, standing nearby, not getting in the way, while a doctor takes care of the patient. The middle of the night duty is even more exhausting when I am not directly engaged with a patient.

One night I get my turn. A little boy is brought in by his parents. He's fallen on broken glass in the house and his knee needs suturing. I am told to take care of it.

PA School

First thing, as I enter the cubicle with the nurse, the young father starts yelling, "I want a real doctor."

I think to myself, *I could just run out the back door.*

But I get started, laying out the needle in preparation for numbing the area, placing the equipment on the sterile pad, trying to appear competent.

The nurse calms the father, and in the most natural voice says to me, "Good, you are keeping the sterile field."

But I wasn't keeping the sterile field, the nurse is saying it to warn me, for my benefit.

When the boy's knee is done and looks decent, I pray in relief. Out of earshot of the family, I wholeheartedly thank the nurse, who is aptly named Angel.

Another day in the ER, a young woman is brought in, shot by her ex-husband with their baby in her arms. The baby is taken to another hospital and survives. The young mother dies on the table in spite of the frantic efforts of the whole team surrounding her. As I look on at her, seeing her pretty flowered bra, I think, "Little did you think when you picked that out to wear this morning..."

From the waiting room comes the cry of her anguished mother. It echoes throughout the department. I'm stunned to see the attending doctor pick up the phone and make a routine call right after. Later I understand, too much to process in the moment.

The finale of the physician assistant training is two preceptorships. We work ten weeks each as a full-time PA in a clinic or at a doctor's private practice. Just like the shorter rotations, we study during it for the test that follows.

After all of it, the tests, the weeks away, and after graduating, I feel like a beached whale, totally played out and exhausted.

The final step is passing National Boards, not due for a couple of months, so I have time to review all I've learned. I soon start my first PA job, on a trial basis on the condition that I pass National Boards.

Chapter 6
Beginnings and Endings

ALONG WITH MY new PA job, I am volunteering one evening a week at Johanna and Mary Beth's clinic, serving uninsured, sometimes homeless people. Their clinic is under the elevated train, where I previously encountered Betty Big Boots. The El, Philadelphians call it. When I take a person's blood pressure and the El passes by, the patient and I know to go into suspended animation. We can't hear each other above its roar.

At the end of every week's evening shift, like tonight, we sit and eat supper together. The soup kitchen next door sends it over. I am basking in being part of their closeness, sharing their laughter and their amazing knowledge. Tonight, Sylvia, a nurse practitioner, and dedicated activist who inspires me, shares a lecture she's heard on the gradations of asthma and the medicines recommended per level. I'm jotting some notes, just to remind myself what to look up to study later, when Mary Beth feeds it back to us whole. She gets it from listening just once!

Mary Beth is a leader and natural organizer. One time she and Johanna landed in a city to discover there was no rental car reserved for them. Late and without transportation to the conference they had flown to attend, Johanna, also a Four on the Enneagram, burst out, "Let's ask God to help us!"

Mary Beth responded, "God's busy, Johanna! There are wars going on!"

Their clinic is a Philadelphia row house. The living room is the reception area with a round, well-used oak table, an old sofa, and a few chairs and some filing cabinets. Here we register patients and assign them to a room and a worker. Farther back are showers for patients, boxes of new underwear and socks stored to give out, and a large, well- organized pharmacy closet. A room with a dentist chair is all the way in back. When I have a patient, I walk with them upstairs to one of three consulting rooms. One night I stand with a patient over the sink while his skin-popping abscesses pour out foul- smelling pus. It's a totally different practice from my upper-class job.

Patients are able to make phone calls to obtain necessary benefits and can call their families. I listen brokenheartedly one night as a homeless father talks to his young son,

"Son, it's your father …. oh yes, I'm happy to hear your voice too." I'm all right … how are you doing?"

It is a safe, welcoming place. Sitting in the waiting room, I overhear patients sharing with each other the names of places to avoid, like shelters with bad reputations, where they'd been robbed and beaten up.

Johanna and I report to each other one night that we received notice that we passed National Boards. I am set in my full-time PA job, a group practice of five internal medicine doctors in a very nice suburb. I do have a long commute from home, over an hour through three hubs of high traffic.

After a few months, I start boarding with a woman near my job a few nights a week. She takes in students. She has an artist living there. He is painting her kitchen ceiling to look like something out of the Sistine Chapel with angels abounding. I am so glad for her clean, quiet room upstairs. I eat Special K out of the box for comfort.

It's hard being a rookie on the job. I often feel, as Johanna put into words, "just behind the curve." But I see patients every day and don't have any disasters. I check with one of the five available doctors if I have the slightest doubt.

One of the doctors, Dr. Walheim, always has time to answer my questions. When I make an important mistake one day, it is to him I go.

"Doc, I just put PPD serum into a patient's upper arm."

I was giving a series of shots; the girl's mother was already acting impatient. I am thorough and careful, but never fast.

Dr. Walheim, a forgiving man, once told me, when I was bemoaning my slowness, "Speed kills."

What I mess up is a PPD test for TB, typically given during a routine physical as this one is, to fulfill pre-college requirements. It's a skin test, to be put shallowly into the patient's inner forearm and checked within forty-eight hours for a reaction. As I work through the young patient's required check list, I give the PPD like the other shots, deep into the upper arm, in the deltoid muscle, where we typically give shots.

I excuse myself from the mother and daughter right after, realizing I've put it in the wrong site. Acting unruffled, I slip out the door, "I just need one more thing," I say, and head straight for Dr. Walheim.

"Well, you've got to tell her."

I go back to the consulting room and tell them.

"I need to redo that last shot. It has to go into the forearm," and I go ahead with it, ignoring the miffed-looking mother and explaining that it will need to be checked in two days.

Typically, I see sinus infections, urinary tract infections, skin rashes, tick bites. And I get to be doctor of the day at the nearby college, calling Dr. Walheim for any high-risk condition, such as a sports injury concussion. I call to double-check signs and symptoms and how long the student needs to be out of play, just to be sure and safe.

Toward the end of my third year there, I look at a little house in the woods, eager to stop the long commute that has me out the door around 7:30 a.m. and often not home until close to 7:30 p.m. The house is a unique little place, quiet, simple, but after a weekend of thinking about it, I let it go. I am thinking about mission with Maryknoll.

I submit an application to Maryknoll, and it's accepted! My mission dream is now firm and clear. I give notice to the doctors and treat myself to several weeks of free time before I am scheduled to start training as a lay missioner. The medical and office staff have a luncheon for me and gift me a passport pouch stuffed with hundreds of dollars.

In short order, I rent a house at the shore for a week of beach and sun. It is heaven, a few steps to the beach. I am letting the quiet and the beauty heal me, as I chase after seagulls and watch sunsets. Afterward, home a few days, I am getting ready to call my friend Pam, who left her watch at the beach house when she visited me there. I figure I'd return it and spend Friday evening with her. Just as I go to pick up the phone, it rings. It's my parents' nursing home.

Beginnings and Endings

"Your mother has taken a turn for the worse," the nurse says. "I'll be right there," I say. I grab a jacket and head for the car.

My sister Helen, who has faithfully taken turns with me visiting our parents in the nursing home, is traveling in Spain with her husband, Mike. My brother John and his wife, Gerri, always caring and responsible, are states away.

I speed the hour south. A nurse has set up an urn of coffee for me to keep vigil by my mother's bedside. It touches me and further confirms for me what is happening.

My mother, tinier than ever, is asleep, hardly a discernible form among the covers. I sit holding her hand. She seems stable. I dash up one floor and bring my father down in a wheelchair.

"You need to say goodbye, Dad."

"Oh, she's all right," he says. "Well, it's a good idea."

I wheel him into her room and wait out in the hall.

After he's had time, I wheel him back up to his room and go back to my mother.

My mother is taking deep breaths. Then her breaths are spaced farther apart. Finally, my mother takes one last deep breath and no more. By then I am leaning forward, arms gently around my mother. When I finally lay her all the way back down, my shirt is soaked with tears.

When I'm ready, I alert the nurse and go up to my father's room and tell him. I sit with him. He is quiet and after a while just staring off. I step out into the hall, looking in without being obvious. He has turned on his stomach and is sobbing.

I called them the Sweethearts in their later years. They took a walk together every day.

They had a well-practiced harmony and seemed to enjoy each other's company. I make sure the nurse on my father's floor is aware of my mother's death and that she'll check in on him.

Before I leave, I take a moment with the night staff on my mother's floor. I thank them for the gift they have given me. There is busyness with several people in my mother's room. I don't go back in. It is about 3 a.m. when I drive home.

I still have a few weeks before I need to report to Maryknoll, and I've arranged to be part of a group of old friends going to Ireland. Soon after my mother's funeral and with my sister home to be with our dad, I go. Ireland is all I hope for: a beautiful country, wonderful people, and our group is full of fun in our rental van. My friend Cathy, notoriously opinionated, keeps saying to her husband, making us all laugh, when he asks a question, "I have no opinion about that."

Cathy and Maggie are my close friends from high school. Maggie and I, the two single-agains, both divorced, share a room in the big house we rent in the Irish countryside with the world's slowest washer/dryer. Maybe we have not put the proper coins in the meter.

In one town we drive to, we each venture out on our own. I'm sitting in a little garden savoring tea and brown bread when the group van pulls up. They are trying to make the ferry to the Aran Islands. I jump in, tea and all. I feel young and free!

When I come back to New Jersey, I just have time to finish clearing out my house to have it ready for the couple who are going to rent it. I store the furniture that I haven't given away over the previous months in a church basement, where my friend Diane's husband, Richard, is the custodian. On the last day, I'm packing one more carload as the family renting my house pulls up. I am soon driving to stay at Diane's house. Early the next morning I start the drive to Maryknoll.

The only things I have responsibility for are packed into my old red Honda Civic. It's an exhilarating feeling of freedom, and I'm soaring as I ride along. I have no desire to be free from my kids, though. Second - guessing myself in the few days before I was to leave, I called each of them, worried they'd feel I was abandoning them.

Trish said, "You know us, Mom, do what you want and stay in close touch."

Jack said, "Mom, I moved to Colorado. I did what I wanted. You get to do what you want."

Remembering their words, cherishing them, I keep driving.

Starting at Maryknoll this August means training in New York until mid-December, then a break of several weeks before leaving the country. I worked it out with my kids that I'll spend time with them before leaving. After the Christmas break with my family, I'll attend language school in Cochabamba, Bolivia. And now I have my assignment, totally unlike Guatemala. I am to be in the Andes Mountains of Peru, at 13,000 feet altitude, living in a village with the indigenous Aymara people.

Chapter 7
Arriving at Maryknoll

AT THE END of several highways, I'm finally driving into Maryknoll's upstate New York town. Now I can open the windows and enjoy the breeze. Passing through quiet streets, nice old houses and trees, I check my written directions one more time for the last few miles. I'll be living here until Christmas, my only responsibility being to take classes preparing for mission work.

Gone is my job as a physician assistant, with its one hour and fifteen-minute commute. My house is rented, furniture safely stored. My kids, now married with full lives of their own, have sent me off with their blessing. The months ahead feel unbelievably simple. I pull into the parking lot in front of the old stone house, previously an early convent for the nuns. I've been here before for the initial interview and psychological testing.

Today it's very quiet. At the end of the downstairs hall of offices, I find my name on a bulletin board just outside the chapel's stained-glass doors. I go in and kneel in the back.

Thank you! This is wonderful!

Upstairs, I look for the name of my assigned partner, *Alexa Reardon*, along the corridor doors. I come upon my own name first, *Lucy Regan*, and step into my new home. In the sunny room there's a single bed, a desk, and a whole wall of shelves. I'm especially happy with the shelves and feel stress fall away as I set up family photos, teas, candles, and books. It's still very quiet, so I roam the building, making my way down to the basement. Tucked in back of the laundry area is a storage space with stacked furniture. I see a comfortable-looking chair, a little table, and a reading lamp and haul them up to my room on the elevator.

Soon after there's a knock on my door and Alexa comes rushing in. We talked on the phone, and I saw a photo of her. In the photo she was laughing, holding up skis. She broke her leg on the slopes later that day, she told me.

But here she is, hands on hips, her blonde hair swinging as she spins her head around. "Whoa, Lucy, my room doesn't look like this!"

She starts laughing, her pretty face brightening even more.

"There's stuff in the basement. I'll help you get some to your room if you want."

I know Alexa's background from talking to her on the phone. I know she is single with a longtime boyfriend, and about a decade and a half younger than me. I know she was raised in New York City, her father a policeman, her mother from Ireland.

She's, ironically, a smoker and a runner. She was a volunteer rape counselor and had a prestigious job as a financial VP at Columbia University. Most of all, my initial sense is that she is fun, easy to know, kind, smart, and savvy.

Chapter 8

Lost in Canada

IN THE DAYS before classes begin, we are invited to two welcoming receptions. The first is a cocktail party at the priests' residence, a beautiful old stone building with a curved Chinese-style roof. Lexi and I are trudging up the hill to attend, and I share what I know about Maryknoll's history.

"I love the style of this building," I tell her. "When Maryknoll started around 1912, the priests first went to China. And I love this part of the history, "The newly organized priests invited young women to join the organization as support staff, to help put out their monthly magazine. But the women soon formed their own religious order of nuns, the Maryknoll Sisters of Saint Dominic, declaring they were going to do overseas mission themselves. Among them was young Molly Rogers, who became their longtime beloved mother superior, Mother Mary Joseph."

Lexi and I pull open the heavy arched wooden doors of the priests' building and walk through the spacious stone floor lobby. Further along, a wide corridor displays class pictures of Maryknoll priests and brothers, fewer in number over each passing year, a sign of the times.

We hear a room buzzing with conversation and go in. The men are cordial and welcoming, asking where we are from and where we're assigned. The snacks and a glass of wine are nice too.

"The brothers," I say on the way back down, "are men doing the same Maryknoll mission work, but not ordained priests."

"Right, I knew that one," Lexi says, perhaps tactfully signaling that she has had enough of my lecture.

The next day we walk up the hill in the other direction to the nuns' convent for their welcoming reception. We are invited to have tea and cookies and meet the sisters. I'm impressed with their lively and informed conversation, including current US politics and world issues.

When we passed through the halls on the way in, I looked at notices for lectures and classes posted outside classrooms, featuring countries Maryknoll serves. We are welcome to all of these, including Spanish lessons, I note, which I can always use.

One sister at the reception seeks me out. "I'm Sister Pat. I served in Peru for many years," she says. "I see you are assigned there." She points at the country name penned on my name sticker.

I glance around for Lexi, but she's across the crowded room. Sister Pat and I start talking. She's in a wheelchair, her hands stiff and misshapen by what looks like a long-standing case of severe rheumatoid arthritis.

"I went to Peru as a young teacher," she tells me.

"I am so looking forward to it," I say, then I add, "I was asked because of earlier newspaper work to write up a piece on the new missioners."

"I'm a writer too, she says, and I'd be glad to work with you on the article."

During the years I was getting an undergraduate degree, I worked in a local newspaper composing room. They had a contract to put out a national trade paper, *The Daily News Record*.

I worked just a couple of late-afternoon hours each day so I could be home to have supper with the kids. I loved the job. One time when we needed to add a late story, I had to dash into the room that housed the giant clanking printer and shout, "Stop the press!"

I had a couple of articles published in the local Sunday magazine when I worked there.

One about the New Jersey Pine Barrens, and the other about the Rescue Mission, a shelter for homeless men. I remember feeling guided to a job that was a perfect fit for me.

Sister Pat and I begin weekly visits at the convent. The nuns' residence is set up in layers. The first floor is a lovely big chapel, and true to their media history, a first-class museum.

The museum has wonderful photos, like the one of the first nuns and Mother Mary Joseph crossing the gangplank of a Chinese junk to start mission there, toting old-fashioned suitcases.

Sister Pat is on the second floor, where the relatively mobile retired nuns live. It's quiet and softly lit. I try to walk carefully down the hall to stop my rubber-soled shoes from squeaking. I see Sister Pat's youthful photo on her door jamb. All the sisters have their photos outside their rooms from their days of service. Sister Pat's shows a tall, willowy young woman. She's lost many inches to arthritis.

In our talks she's engaging and warm-hearted, laughing easily, making me laugh. A nun friend pops in with a quick message, and she tells me Sister Pat often wheels around and leaves little candy treats at their doors.

"She's getting us all fat," she laughs.

The third floor is essentially a nursing home. It's touching to see the youthful photos outside those doors with the sisters inside so diminished. Yet they are home, in the home of all their lives, and being well cared for by the nuns in that service. On one visit I walk around the back garden and see the sisters' cemetery, ranging from nuns who've died many years ago to recent deaths. A Blessed Mother statue in her grotto watches over them all.

On one visit Sister Pat gives me advice about the article I'm writing, "Tell them what you're going to say, say it, tell them you said it."

This is Sister Pat: clear, real to her fingertips, helpful. We discover we are both Fours on the Enneagram, a personality type system, the topic I enjoyed listening to on the Richard Rohr cassette tapes driving back and forth to work. Fours are creative and crave beautiful aesthetics in their lives. Sister Pat said I'd love the beauty of Peru and its people. I certainly loved her. The piece I'm writing," Introducing Our New Missioners," is for Maryknoll's monthly magazine, the same little *Reader's Digest* sized magazine I had pored over on the trolley as a teenager.

In mission prep classes, we have some lecturers from the International Monetary Fund and the World Bank. They teach us to be realistic about what is possible to achieve in a few years of service. Infrastructure, years in the making, needs to be in place for some projects, they say.

Other experienced missioners come and share helpful lessons from their experiences. One woman tells us her neighbors would knock on her door and ask her to bake them a cake for their child's birthday.

Her first thought, "*Es mi casa. Y soy una enfermera.*" "This is my home, and I'm a nurse!" But then, "If this is how I can connect with the people, then this is part of my mission."

The overall focus of our training is learning to identify community needs and strategies to break down structural injustice. We talk too about culture shock and how to manage it. What I take from that is to be aware of myself, pay attention to my extreme behavior. One priest says, "Look for signs like piling heaping spoonfuls of sugar in your coffee, or getting habitually irritable, angry, and critical."

One evening a week, a delightful respite, I sing in our little house choir. And I continue to meet with Sister Pat well past the completion of the article. I'm taking the Spanish class.

On Labor Day weekend, I'm driving back to Maryknoll after a visit with my father, who is alone now in the nursing home with my mother gone. I try to visit at least every other weekend. Tonight, I am hopelessly lost on the way back. When I see a sign for Canada, I'm close to tears. I'm feeling lost in a strange place and afraid and chastising myself in the bargain.

To further compound it, nothing is open on the Sunday of Labor Day weekend. I can't pop into a store and ask for directions. Finally, I see a diner open and walk in. I see a man at a booth near the door and ask for directions.

"I'm a cab driver," he says, "If you wait for me to finish, you can follow me right there."

Having seen the sign for Canada, I am desperate. I agree, and in a little bit I am following his lit-up cab sign. In minutes, we pull into Maryknoll's driveway.

"Thank you!" I am already acting like the nuns with no money. I promise I'll pray for him.

Kind soul that he is, he seems happy enough with that.

I come in through the back entrance, past the computer room where two of our guys are huddled over a computer. It feels like home, and they feel like brothers, waving and telling me Lexi is looking for me. As I walk toward my room, Lexi is coming down the hall.

"We were worried about you. You never come back this late!"

When I tell her about seeing the Canada sign, she bursts out laughing, "Luuucy!" she says, doing her Ricky Ricardo imitation.

Sometimes we go to rent a movie with a few others, engaging in endless debates in the video store about which movie to choose. Finally, back at Bethany, our house, we gather with a group in the little sitting room at the end of the hall to watch, munching bowls of popcorn we make in the kitchen on our floor.

As summer ends, I am beguiled by the Hudson Valley autumn. Lexi and I are becoming friends. Today we're walking along the Hudson, Lexi smoking, and us always bubbling with good conversation and laughter. Laughter, as I'd express it later in my journal, as bright as the colors of the glorious trees.

Lexi and I share the Irish heritage of the love of language. The Irish would say we make good *craic*, a Gaelic word meaning good fun talk. On this walk we discover we have the same favorite book, "*A Prayer for Owen Meany.*"

Over shared meals, classes, and group trips our class of about two dozen is growing closer. We all pile in a bus to New York City today and attend a session at the UN, using translating headphones up in the balcony to hear what is being said on the floor below. I'm thrilled to be here, but the people on the floor are so unhurried. I was expecting urgency; *don't they know the state of crisis in the world?!*

A longer trip another day is to Fort Benning, The School of the Americas, in Columbus, Georgia. It has the reputation of teaching violent tactics to Latin American soldiers to force cooperation on their own people. We've made posters to protest this and to remember the names of those killed by this program.

The next morning, we start with Mass and then march through the gate and into the fort, which is considered trespassing and is forbidden. I'm marching along, holding the name of a mother and her two children, which is certainly hitting home to me. We say their names as our turn comes, then in unison we say, ¡Presente! Present! Their souls are present and remembered.

After the march we gather to be bussed to a meeting place for the whole group to return to Maryknoll. The bus comes and we board. A soldier enters and places a plastic band on our wrists. I'm puzzled and even more so when we are driving further into the fort and not to the exit. We are let off at a large tent. It has rained so our folding chairs are set among puddles.

Rumor drifts back to us about the bus that went ahead of us. We are being taken to a kind of court. We are to be charged, possessions confiscated. I slip my favorite peace sign pin to a zipped pocket inside my jacket.

I worry, *Will this affect my physician assistant license?*

Eventually we are detained in a large lecture hall. One by one we are called forth and handed an official looking paper.

As we finally board our bus for home, I again study my "sentence." Banned and barred from entering Fort Benning for five years.

All of us take turns cooking dinner during our time in training. The guys sometimes order pizza for the group on their night.

Our favorite night is Coralis's turn. She makes a Filipino dish: spring rolls with a delicious chicken and rice casserole. Nobody is absent for Coralis's night.

Lexi and I sometimes do the big food shop with everybody's chipped-in money and their list. One time, Russ, a serious young guy in our group, says he'll go with us. Lexi is driving and at one point realizes she isn't sure how to get to the store. We both get lost on a regular basis.

"Lucy, roll down the window," she says at a red light," Ask that guy." I quickly ask the guy in the car beside us before the light changes.

As I am asking, I hear Russ sounding awestruck in the back, saying, "Can you *do* that?" To us, both from big cities on the East Coast, this is common practice.

"People do it all the time where we live," we say.

We love telling that story and break up laughing with every re-telling. "Can you *do* that?"

Another time Russ is walking up to the front porch of our group house as I am returning from helping out in the vegetable garden behind the father's infirmary. We bring the food weekly to a church that distributes it to families. I show him three delicious-looking tomatoes for tonight's supper that I retrieved from where they had fallen to the ground, just slightly bruised.

He says, "Stealing from the needy, that's a slippery slope."

Our favorite story: Lexi invites her then-boyfriend for the weekend, and she must sign a form at the office for her weekend's absence. The supervisor asks her, "What's your friend's name?"

Lexi, dumbstruck, quickly makes up a name, Helen Granahan. The next week, we are playing a pull-a-name-out-of-a-hat group game with one of the leaders. Someone put in the name Helen Granahan.

"Who's that?" the leader asks. We all try to look genuinely puzzled and don't dare make eye contact with each other, laughter just a breath away.

One evening Derek calls. He's the husband of the couple we are replacing in Peru. He is visiting in New York and wants to meet with us. He's a big, authoritative guy. Over pizza, he is talking about our new home. He begins describing how we'll be next door to them, sharing their outhouse. I gulp, maybe for the first time taking in the reality of what I am facing. I can't think straight.

"Lexi," I say, "we've got to go, we have that thing." She looks at me, gets it, and quickly agrees.

"Oh, right, yes, we'll be late."

We fly out of there, not talking much on our way home.

That night I dream I am in Cape May, New Jersey, a place where my kids and I loved to vacation. I am walking along the street of Victorian houses that face the ocean. In the dream there is an on-ramp, and I walk up it. As I round the ramp's ascending curve and turn onto the flat, elevated road, a thick mist engulfs me. I can't tell the ocean from the sky, can't see my feet or the road ahead of me. There are thin steel uprights about three feet apart along the railing, like rebar jutting out of unfinished buildings. I hold on to each one as I walk forward. "Mother of God," I keep saying. I am terrified.

· · · · ·

We end our last few weeks at Maryknoll with a volley of vaccinations, everything from malarial shots to prophylaxis injections against rabies in case of dog bites.

We also take a psychological test, and Lexi and I are sitting together in front of the director today to get the results.

"You two are very compatible," she says. "Your personalities complement each other.

You'll do fine in the field. Only drawback: you both have a terrible sense of direction."

During our final week we are scheduled for practice for the Maryknoll traditional sending ceremony. Former missioners whose commitment has been in the same country will bless us and send us off. One afternoon we are reporting for rehearsal at the big chapel up the hill in the priests' building. It's a beautiful chapel where I've attended concerts and Masses. We are all trooping up as a class when Lexi whispers to me, "Lucy, where is the big chapel exactly?" She is irreverent, charmingly conniving, kind, and funny, the perfect mission partner for me.

Chapter 9
Family Visits – Language School

LEAVING MARYKNOLL, the whole gang gathers in the parking lot, cheering each other off. Several drive around the parking lot once before driving on, but for some reason, unwittingly, I drive around the whole building. Embarrassed at myself, I am cheered by their good-natured laughter as I head for the highway.

First stop, my daughter, Trish, and her husband, Rod, in Maryland. The plan is to sell my car during my visit here, then fly to Colorado to spend the second part of the holiday with my son, Jack, and his wife, Jane. After that I'll head to Cochabamba, Bolivia, for Maryknoll's Language school.

At Rod and Trish's, I try virtual reality glasses for the first time. When I see a giant whale looming out of the ocean at me, I drop them. Too real, too scary!

Rod loves electronic gadgets, and I am more comfortable playing air guitar when he gives me a lesson on this device. Mostly we're talking and laughing. I love Trish's stories of the early grade school kids she teaches at her Montessori school.

One kid, when answering a math question, rubbed his chin, and said, "I'd have to say…" Trish said to him, "This isn't a quiz show, Anthony."

Rod is telling me about his adventures playing Ultimate

Frisbee, and I'm appreciating team sports through him. I feel welcomed and loved.

When I get to Colorado we go to the elegant Broadmoor Hotel, where my son used to work as an audio/video tech. We toast each other with wine in the hotel's elegant lounge. Jack, Jane, and I are looking out the French doors at the snow falling softly on the hotel's lake.

One quiet evening, a few nights later, Jane, loving and practical and easygoing, is enjoying a movie. Jack is out in his brew shack, and I am up in my room reading. I feel a deep peace. I am blessed with having the family I always wanted. Open, showing their caring in action, and living rich, independent lives. I put down my book and breathe deeply. Maybe part of my incentive to work at helping others is that I have been so abundantly loved and blessed, and I want to thank God with action.

After the delight of hanging out with my kids, I am off to Cochabamba. In "Coche," as the nuns and priests stationed here call it, I know I can easily keep in touch with my family by email in the city's many cybercafés. We'll live with Spanish-speaking families and attend Spanish class daily from January until we leave for Peru, several months later.

The mission couple we are replacing, Derek and Suzanne, come to meet Lexi and me soon after we arrive in Cochabamba. Ever cautious, I am prepared for the cold climate of the Andes with long underwear under my jeans and a jacket. The couple is taking us out to dinner. Lexi and I are in the back of the cab.

"This is a warm country!" Derek turns and says, "Why do you have a coat on?"

I mumble something polite to him and whisper to Lexi, "I'm actually having hyperthermia." She starts laughing. I try to stop laughing, but we burst out again as we ride along, gawking at everything new. The dinner is good. Lexi and I ask a lot of questions about where we're going. I enjoy the spaghetti and slip off my outer layers.

For the duration of language school, I'm assigned to board with an older widow. She's lived for decades in her large, gracious house and often has company, a living room full of well-mannered older folk. The custom is that as you enter a room, each person must be greeted with a kiss on the cheek. There is no slipping by in the hallway, as much as I want to dash upstairs and get to my homework.

We start language classes right away, four hours a day. Each session is a group of four students per cubicle with the teachers rotating so we hear different accents and experience different methods of learning. Some teachers push us to give quick answers in a lively quiz; some engage us in conversation, however slow and stumbling on our end.

Missioners from other organizations also attend Maryknoll's language school, some from as far away as England and Ireland. Our sense of community develops quickly. We're all in this together. We laugh at our frequent mistakes and meet up on the avenue for coffee and ice cream. We have a simple Mass at the end of the school day, and we troop up the hill together, enjoying the balmy weather for which I now dress appropriately.

During one Mass, a Maryknoll sister gets up and says she has a sad announcement. "Sister Pat has been in the hospital as she was no longer able to eat. She died yesterday afternoon."

I walk back down the hill with the sister, heavy-hearted.

Sister tells me that when Sister Pat reached the stage of being unable to eat, her last pleasure, she said, "I *do* mind," unlike her heroic attitude through all the rest of her losses and suffering.

I cherish having known her, my beloved writing tutor and pal. On our last visit she gave me a crucifix necklace that her students from Peru had brought to her on a visit to the US. I protested, "Oh, Pat, this is too precious to you."

"No," she said, "It's your turn now."

It's Saturday, Lexi and I are walking to our favorite outdoor restaurant. We always get empanadas, beefy and juicy in a warm, chewy crust. Afterward we take the long way home. It's always beautiful weather here and good to be outside. We look out for the large, loose concrete pavement block that we have learned the hard way goes violently askew if stepped on, splashing muddy water on us.

I go to a *futbol* game with a few other students, thrilled to see the players doing their amazing maneuvers in person. One player, long hair flying, does a 180-degree turn a few feet from us at the foul line. Then he somehow toes the ball back into play. We're laughing and cheering and clapping.

Melvina, my hostess, has a young Aymara woman working for her. Celia has a tiny room across the back patio. She eats alone in the kitchen after preparing our meals. She also cleans the house, weeds and waters the garden, and washes the car. It raises my social justice hackles.

I help her enroll in a computer class, but Melvina says Celia can't attend because she herself must be out those evenings, and the house can't be left with no one home. Though the houses in the neighborhood are nice, very upper class, they have high fences with broken glass on top, and often with snarling dogs leaping and barking when people (us) walk by.

I say I'll stay home so Celia can attend. That works for a few nights of classes, but when I see that Celia's lessons consist of copying the introduction to the instruction book word for word, both the student and her "rescuer" give up. I have a lot to learn. And I obviously have not learned the cardinal rule, that is, not to bully one's ideas into another's culture.

One student in our language classes is a strong fundamental Christian. When the group posts an invitation for a little gathering early in Holy Week, the week before Easter, she tears it off the bulletin board in a rage.

"You people are sacrilegious," she cries.

Soon after, on the patio outside the classrooms, vendors arrive selling local wares. One item I can't help noticing is a huge hat made from brown beaver fur, roughly the size of a manhole cover. The next day our woman walks in with it on. I nod toward the hat walking by. My beautiful young Irish classmate says, "Aye, it's desperate!" We muffle our laughter.

I often walk out on Sunday with a priest friend, Paul, from England. We walk and walk through the crowded indoor markets with intriguing merchandise and peek into antique stores along the streets. We wind up with coffee and pastry each time in a different café. He saves me many a lonely Sunday. I tease him about how he mangles Spanish with his English accent.

La Paaaz, he says, rhyming with *jazz,* when giving the "Peace be with you" at Mass, instead of *La Pahz,* like the *ah* in father.

One time a kid at Mass looks quizzically at him, wondering why he was saying the name of the city in Bolivia, La Paz. But the boy goes along with him and answers with the name of another Peruvian city, "Arequipa."

Once a week I assist a doctor in his clinic near language school. I don't contribute much, but I get some medical language practice and learn the Spanish names of some common medicines.

On a walk I discover a camp of homeless people living near the monument to Cochabamba women warriors, high up on a hill, surrounded by woods. I go back, bringing a few friends, and talk with the people. A young mother with a baby is among the group. A couple of the guys, Paul and another young priest, and I collect potatoes, bread, peanut butter, and bottled water and bring it up to them a few days later. The young mother quietly accepts the food with no fanfare, but we feel better.

Because I studied Spanish for years, I know the basics and it serves me well. I am making progress and using it whenever I can, but another female student around my age explodes in frustration.

"How do they expect me to learn if they only speak Spanish in class?!"

Later she loses her temper with a cab driver and pounds on his back fender for not picking us up. One of the fathers, Father Gorky, asks me to speak to her.

I walk over to where she is staying.

"If I stay angry," she tells me, "I don't fall into depression."

She had lost a grandchild in a fire. The unimaginable. Now it all makes sense. She seems relieved to tell the truth about what has been going on with her.

The finale of language school is reciting a memorized paragraph before the assembled students and teachers. We all stumble through it. Genuine fluency is hard won.

After language school, Lexi and I fly to Arequipa as a stop on the way to Lima, where we are slated to meet Derek for orientation before going up to our site in the *Altiplano*, Peru's high planes.

Arequipa is an old colonial city, at an altitude of five thousand feet, about that of Denver. The nuns advised us to take a few days there as acclamation for changing altitudes. Lima is at sea level; Cochabamba is around eight thousand feet.

We are flying into Arequipa, soon before landing, when I am astonished to be facing the side of a mountain, seemingly a few feet away!

"Should I be able to see pebbles that clearly on the side of that mountain?" I ask Lexi. She looks up from her book and looks out, then looks back at me wide eyed.

We later get used to flying close to what we learn is the volcano, Misti, when landing at Arequipa. Once the capital of Peru, Arequipa lost that distinction when the capital was moved to Lima, likely because of volcanic eruptions

We stay a few days at *La Casa De Mi Abuela*, The House of My Grandmother. It is mostly a big, sun-drenched garden dotted with a lot of little cabins. They are tiny rooms but private, clean, and comfortable. And they serve coffee with pancakes and fresh fruit in the morning in the garden.

We explore Arequipa, a lovely city. We pass through little parks, a real downtown, and a beautiful colonial plaza, *El Parque Central*, where we have coffee on one of the balconies overlooking the plaza. We hear music and look over the railing to see a parade circling below trumpets blaring.

Nearby is a store with the best chocolate ever. We visit an old convent, now a museum, a rambling place with dark, echoing stone halls. The nuns' private quarters have iron gates at their entry. The wealthier women, likely the eldest daughter assigned by their family to be the designated nun, have an extra room inside for a servant girl.

After a few days we fly to Lima. Men in traditional clothes are playing lilting music on pan flutes to greet travelers at the airport. I feel like dancing. We are in good spirits as we get in a van and head for the Maryknoll Center.

The center, where several Maryknoll priests live, has rooms for visitors. We say hello to the fathers and head to our rooms, done for the day.

Chapter 10
Town Mouse, Country Mouse

I WAKE UP feeling luxurious in one of the center's comfortable, dark-paneled rooms. I'm in Lima, Peru! I quickly pull on clothes and head for Lexi's room down the carpeted hall. She's awake, having a smoke on her room's balcony, leaning on the railing.

"This is nice, huh?" she says.

Downstairs we have a less travel-weary look at the Maryknoll Center, a rambling house in the upscale Miraflores district of Lima. It's the home of several Maryknoll fathers who I know from their visits to New York, men I like for their down-to-earth friendliness and helpfulness.

We're greeted with a full breakfast, with choices, served in the big, bright dining room by two ample, apron-clad Peruvian women. They laugh as we ooh and ahhh at their sumptuous offerings.

"*¡Ustedes eran muy flaco, toma dos salchichas!*" "You two are very skinny, take two sausages."

We're having fun bantering with them. We're ladies of leisure on vacation.

After eating we head to our orientation appointment with Derek. The house's interior garden is visible from where we sit at a table with him in the library, and my attention is drawn to the view of the lush plants in the sunny atrium. Like the chapel that I peeked into on the way, the library has sturdy blond furniture and beautiful Peruvian rugs. I'm feeling peaceful.

Derek begins by reading to us from the Maryknoll manual. "Maryknoll is a round table organization, not hierarchical," he reads.

I think, but don't say, *I can read, Derek.*

After we are done with the manual, he suggests an excursion to downtown Lima, lecturing us as we head out of the Center House to be on guard for pickpockets. Lexi, having lived all her life in Manhattan, flashes me a quick eye roll. Derek walks fast, a half block ahead of us. We lag behind, adjusting to crossing major streets with no traffic lights. Lexi holds her arm straight out with her hand held up and the cars stop, a New York move I intend to learn. We were surprised to hear that there are no traffic lights in Lima, a city with a Starbucks and modern department stores and casinos. "It's an old city, too expensive to retrofit," one of the fathers had told us.

We look up from talking to see Derek huffing and puffing back to us. He says his watch has been lifted from his arm! We're sorry for him. He's upset, of course, but when we're on our own later, we can't help but be struck by the irony.

That afternoon, Lexi and I walk to the Pacific Ocean, a few long blocks away. We pass the Japanese Embassy, the site of Ann Patchett's novel "*Bel Canto*", based on an actual siege of the embassy when hostages were held for months.

When we get to the ocean rolling and crashing below the high cliffs, I think of how far I am from the familiar Atlantic Ocean on the Jersey shore. We watch people jump off the two-story-high cliff with parasails, floating over the ocean breezes.

They're attached to the large, curved kites by only a sit-in harness. They run to the edge of the cliff, jump off, and fly into mid-air! I consider myself emotionally daring. I went to PA school in my fifties and signed up for foreign mission, but I have zero daring for that kind of physical bravery.

We walk away from the coast along a wide boulevard lined with palm trees and several other elegant foreign embassy facades. After a few long blocks, alongside light traffic, we spot a restaurant with outdoor tables and go onto the terrace. The polite older waiter welcomes us. I'm swooning in ambiance heaven.

"Maybe," we say, chatting over coffee, trying to be understanding, "Derek is used to younger missioners with less life experience, some who'd welcome more guidance."

I am in my late fifties, Lexi in her early forties. To be fair to him, most of the missioners in our home group are in their twenties or thirties.

We're loving our time in Lima; it's warm and at sea level. But soon enough we're packing to go to Puno, our assigned mission site, high in the Andes.

The next morning when we're flying there, I ask Lexi, "How do you think thirteen hundred feet altitude will feel."

"We are going to find out very soon," she says. "Do we have coca tea?"

"I got it." I show her the little pouch. Several Maryknollers recommended we buy coca tea, known to quell altitude sickness.

Derek and his wife, Suzanne, meet us at the Maryknoll Center House in Puno when we arrive by jitney from the airport. Suzanne has gathered a group of Aymara women in their full skirts and long braids in the house garden to greet us. The women rain flower petals down on us, a traditional greeting. We are all laughing, awash in flowers and the sheer newness!

Afterward we pile into the missioners' truck and drive the main road to their village, where we will all live for now. Lexi and I are taking in the fields, the cows, the adobe houses. On our left, a ribbon of Lake Titicaca sparkles. There are no road signs, no stores, just fields of some kind of crops, and in the background, huge blue mountains.

We pull into their yard and have a quick look at their place: bedroom, a low bed covered by a sturdy blanket, big kitchen, dimly lit, featuring a large table, a cookstove, and shelves of pots and pans.Rubber boots with a few flakes of dry mud are lined up atop newspapers by the door.

"Come see the clinic."

This I'm eager for. I'll be working with Suzanne, a nurse practitioner. The clinic is a small, narrow building with a packed dirt floor. Rough shelves are crammed with boxes of various medicines with Spanish names, along with exam gloves, thermometers, and plastic basins.

"We'll see patients outside," Suzanne says. "It's warmer in the sun." "Let me show you your rooms."

Lexi says, "Don't worry, it's up top, right?" She gestures to the house they had pointed out to us when we pulled in. We walk over, waving thanks as Suzanne calls after us, "Dinner in half an hour."

Our rooms are the second story of an Aymara family's house, reached by a handmade ladder. I look back halfway up and can see Derek and Suzanne's home just across the way. A lone outhouse stands between our two dwellings.

Up the roughhewn ladder is a cement deck. Lexi and I are both tired. We each quickly choose one of the two rooms. My space is one large room divided by a wall of apple crates stuffed with old papers. Past this divide, I step across the worn wooden floor to a bed with a table and lamp, a desk, and a metal-trimmed window that I creak open. I like it. It's quiet. It has everything I need, and I can clean out the small entry area to make a cooking space.

As we're unpacking in our rooms, I hear a ruckus below. I pop out onto the patio just as Lexi does.

"What was that?!"

Then we see a donkey below in an enclosure by the next house, bawling away. We are a long way from home.

Early the next morning I'm sitting on the sunny patio on a rolled-up blanket. From my perch I can see the one paved road a distance below. Otherwise, there are only misty fields surrounded by rock walls. I'm in biblical times, seeing villagers passing by, walking with measured gait, tapping their cows' rumps with switches, carrying loads of reeds on their heads.

Lexi is having a smoke in her doorway, away from the wind. We are waiting as instructed for the kitchen door to Derek and Suzanne's house to open to get coffee. I've been down once, door closed. When I climb back up, no coffee. I tell Lexi, "I'm depressed."

"Who wouldn't be depressed in this butt-awful place?" she says, flipping her ash. We start laughing. We can do this. Certainly, we can do this together.

Later that day I make my room comfortable, clearing and cleaning it, then setting up things I brought with me. I start emptying my suitcase. Trish made me a calendar featuring different family photos for each month. I sit on the bed and leaf through the pictures: the kids dressed for Halloween from the big costume bag pressed into service every year. There's us making a vegetable garden; Jack with his floppy hair, a big smile, wielding a hoe. Us at Christmas, us on the beach, Trish, a young teen, posing.

At the bottom of my clothes, I discover a framed print of Van Gogh's *Café Terrace at Night*, my favorite. I pointed it out to Trish in a store on a walk in their neighborhood on our recent visit. She slipped it into my bag.

As the weeks go by, I work with Suzanne in her weekly clinic. It's a huge help to work with someone experienced in the types of medical needs presented and the Aymara ways.

Lexi is looking into a place in another village, one closer to Puno. She hopes to be living where the ancient cathedral is located, where women take a bus from several villages to be together to sew sweaters and make crafts. She plans to upgrade it to a Women's Cooperative with export sales to the US. But for now, she is in the room next to mine.

One morning has a different feel as we climb down the wobbly ladder and head next door. Smoke from breakfast fires makes a haze over the fields. A rooster crows far away. Derek and Suzanne have left for New York for their annual medical check. We have the couples' truck and their big kitchen. I pat the old truck on the way over, it's black paint morphed to a bruised purple.

Our agenda today is to organize the yearly All Saints' Day gathering. People will come to honor their dead. Derek has set up an altar, and the local priest, Father Anuncio, will celebrate Mass. The father, we've been told, will expect lunch. I'm wrapped in an apron, making chicken soup using a recipe learned from Derek, an excellent cook. Lexi is outside receiving the local folks, mostly women.

She comes into the kitchen. "Smells good," she says, "I asked a couple of the kids to lunch."

I nod okay.

"Well, I asked them all."

Oh! I hope we have enough. I'm thinking out loud. "Well, I bought a lot of bread."

I pile up the hollow triangles of bread on a platter. It's sold everywhere, ten for a Peruvian sole, 33cents US.

"And I bought cookies. We'll be okay"

Just then, Father Anuncio roars into the yard in his Jeep. Lunch is on. I peek out to see him checking out the altar. Lexi guides the children in. They come in shyly, their cheeks chapped and ruddy as always from the cold air. Their dark hair is sleek. They're beautiful.

I'm remembering an old Irish priest, Father Michael Doyle, in a church in Camden near where I volunteered in the clinic before PA school. I was attending a First Communion Mass in his parish. The kids, mostly Latino, were walking solemnly down the aisle, scrubbed and shining, hair slicked, collars a little big, pants a little short.

Father Michael said, "When you ask your parents how you were on this day, they can tell you, "You were *perfect*."

That's how I'm seeing these kids.

Once seated, the kids are beaming at each other around the table. Reaching for bread, they relish the soup and are all smiles as they look around the big kitchen. Father Anuncio does not look pleased. Maybe he thinks having lunch with the little neighborhood hooligans is undignified.

But the kids are happy, and us too. I think we're feeling more acclimated and competent.

Most of the people have arrived by the time the last clean dish is put away. Lexi and I head for the yard. I look out, surveying the scene, pushing my hair out of my face.

"Guess I don't have time for a cigarette, right?" she says. We laugh and walk out.

The Aymara folks, always reserved, don't know us. We want to make this All Saints' Day nice, this day when people remember and mourn their dead. We needn't worry... the local folks know the ritual well. They have walked to Suzanne's familiar clinic house, the women in wide felt skirts, derby hats, and shawls laying flowers wrapped in plastic at the altar. Suzanne has been there for them for years.

We gently insert ourselves right in the middle of the group. I feel honored to be hemmed in by them, smelling their country smells, their fields and smoky cook fires. Mourning my own mother, gone just over a year, I tear up. A dry hand reaches for mine.

I get smiles and shoulder pats, so does Lexi.

At the end of the service, after saying goodbye and thank you to all, we head back up to our rooms, talking about how great the truck will be for the shopping we plan: two-burner propane stoves and big canisters of propane, some dishes and sheets. And we're excited for the trip we plan to take tomorrow to see more of the area now that we have wheels.

Chapter 11
Up The High Mountains

NEXT MORNING we're sitting in the truck, turning the map around in our hands. The map, designed for tourists, is more cartoon art than road details. We only know the road to Puno, and now we plan to go to a Maryknoll sisters' town much higher up in the mountains. Sister Camilla asked us to visit her community on All Souls Day when we met her recently at the Center House in Puno.

"I think you go to Puno, then turn left," Lexi says, pointing at the map. "Remember how steep the incline is up that road? It's heading up into the mountains."

I think for a moment, the truck rumbling.

"Since we're going to Puno, why don't we stop at the priests' house and get some basic directions?"

We do and afterward wind up having coffee at our favorite - and only - local coffee shop, studying the real map the fathers have given us, along with advice, cautions, and fatherly suggestions.

"Don't even think about driving once it's dark up there."

"You have food and water with you right?" says plump Father Paul as he offers bananas and rolls.

Savoring the last sip of cafe con leche, I say, "You're right, Lexi, it's the road out of Puno.

Here's the road Father Bob pointed out."

Off we go. As we climb, it gets more rugged, more desolate, with a few scattered dwellings. Boulders here and there define the road. I'm trying to decide, am I more scared to be the driver on this narrow mountain road or more terrified looking out the window from the passenger seat seeing how close we are to the edge?

After an hour of driving, we are thoroughly lost. We've been climbing steadily, but there's no sign of the large town where it should be.

"Is it okay to knock on a hut and ask?"

"Probably not a great idea," I say, laughing. We look at the map again, turning it around.

"We're here, right?" says Lexi, pointing to a spot on the map.

"Right."

"Okay, it's got to be up there. Back there is Puno; over there is Bolivia." More laughing. "Well, that pins it right down."

Still laughing at the vision of us pulling up to an Aymara dwelling, I say, "Remember Russ? When we were lost trying to find the supermarket near Maryknoll, and you said to ask the guy in the car beside us when we stopped at a red light?"

Lexi jumps in. "Can you *do* that?" We both laugh as we remember.

Before another hour passes, we find Sister Camilla's mountain town. The ancient cathedral is being remodeled. We see wooden scaffolding framing its gray stones as we park in the plaza in front. Men are sitting on the low steps before the big double doors of the entrance, just sitting.

Maybe on lunch break, it is midday. I can envision the same scene in the distant past. Different clothes, but I feel like I'm stepping into an illustration in one of my Spanish textbooks.

Up the High Mountains

Sister Camilla appears at her door in the shadow of the cathedral. She waves us over enthusiastically. Sister's mission partner, another Maryknoll nun, has recently left. Camilla is happy for company. We know that from talking with her at the Center House. Tiny, wearing a skirt and simple blouse, with silver hair capping her animated face, Sister leads us into the kitchen. After bread and soup, she takes us on a tour of the cathedral to see the refurbishing in progress.

We walk through the vast space with massive columns. Statues are in shadows in alcoves. Upstairs we peek into simple sleeping rooms off the balcony for visiting priests. When complete, it will serve as a central gathering place for group baptisms and community processions. In a storage room on the ground floor, we spot a Blessed Mother statue on a float with carrying poles, ready for the next procession.

By late afternoon, the people arrive for the All Souls Day ceremony in the old part of the cathedral. Gathered together, they are solemn in the swirling mists as Sister swings a thurible on a chain, wafting incense over the bundles the people have laid inside the altar.

"It's the clothes of their deceased family members," she whispers to us. Our evening together passes in gentle conversation.

Next morning we pack up our few things. Sister Camilla has made pastries to add to our supplies. First, we stroll with her around the village. We walk along the dirt roads greeting folks, seeing women with woven shawls tied over their backs with chubby babies nestled inside. We pass simple adobe houses and walk out onto a lookout, where we see terraced fields carved into the steep hills.

Sister points, "The terraces were created by the first Indian settlers to help manage the steep landscape."

In the morning light we watch men and women hoeing and packing dirt around their plants; the *campesinos* (farmers) are themselves tethered by ropes to the hillside.

Finally, we hug goodbye, promising to visit in Puno whenever we hear Sister is coming. A replacement sister has been delayed in coming. We know it's hard on Camilla. We watch her as we leave, waving and waving as she grows smaller and smaller through the back window.

Next, we're on our way to a convent of nuns that on the map appears to be on a downward sloping road out of Sister's town. We can see just a ribbon of Lake Titicaca glistening far below. One of our Maryknoll sister friends said it would be nice to visit another order of nuns.

On a flat, grassy spot we park and climb up on a flat boulder. We eat our pastries and take pictures of each other, savoring our freedom, savoring just being there. We are pleased with ourselves when we successfully arrive at the next convent. It has a fenced courtyard around a more modern-looking building. A young sister comes out and shows us into a room near the entrance.

"Please wait here," she says.

As I look around the quiet reception room with its polished linoleum floor and the few neatly placed armchairs and tables, I remember having toyed with the idea of becoming a nun when I was in high school. This room, this atmosphere, feels confining. I remind myself that I would have chosen to join a medical mission order, which could very well have been Maryknoll, which meant adventure and engagement. My thoughts are interrupted by an older sister coming into the room.

"Well, how nice," she says, "We always want to meet the new lay missioners."

Lexi chats. She's good at being at ease, letting words flow. Her background working as head of Resources for New York's Columbia University shows. We are led into the dining room and served a chicken and rice dish and meet all the sisters, who bob their heads politely at us. We aren't planning to stay past midafternoon, so we just sit at the table, chatting about our work and our plans for the communities near Puno.

Lexi talks about her planned Women's Cooperative, and I say I want to open a clinic. "Yes, I heard you were a physician assistant," the mother superior says, and to my surprise adds, "I lined up a few patients for you."

While Lexi does Lord knows what, I see the few people, all women, lined up outside a separate building that is the clinic. As it turns out, there are no Aymara women among the group. And no real sickness. I take the blood pressures of the nicely dressed *mestizo* ladies. (a kind of upper-class hierarchy: people of mixed race: European and Indian.)

I advise a few of them to double-check with their doctor, as their blood pressure is slightly elevated. They are very appreciative, seemingly enjoying the novel experience. We soon say goodbye and are back on the road, aware that we need to be back to our village before dark. We almost make it, encountering huge trucks in the early dusk that as always don't dim their headlights when passing. But by then we are approaching the little rutted turnoff into our village. In we go, jolting and swaying.

• • • • •

Next morning, we bring coffee we made in the kitchen up to our concrete porch. We are looking over the fields. It's a misty, peaceful morning. A rooster crows. I've grown to enjoy the sound.

There's something I want to ask Lexi, and this is a good time.

"Lexi, there's a lady in a village along the road to Puno with breast cancer," I start. "Sister Marie told me about her. Would you help me get her to a doctor in Puno?"

I mentioned the patient to Dr. Aponte when I was there with another patient, and he said he'd have to see her to help.

I met Sister Marie at the Center House, the meeting place for all the missioners in our area.

Her mother superior, Sister Francesca, is practical and knowledgeable. She's been giving us housing ideas. Marie is in charge of a small group of young Aymara women who are postulants; that is, in training to be nuns. Marie, also a nurse practitioner, lives just down the hill from the main convent of Sister Francie, as we've come to call her. There Marie has a clinic.

I checked with her before thinking I might rent nearby to Sister Francie, as I didn't want to intrude on her practice. Sister Marie said she'd be fine with the idea, that we could cover for each other when one of us was away.

Lexi, as usual, is ready to help, so we drive to the sick woman's house. Her name is Felipe.

She is in her bed, strained looking, in pain. Her two young daughters hover over her, their long braids brushing the bed as they talk softly to their mother.

All we have is an army blanket from the truck, so we carry Felipe out in it and lay her gently on the back seat. Her daughters, looking just past adolescence, wave goodbye, looking anxious. We assure them we'll get medicine for their mother. Because the girls know the Maryknoll sisters, they trust us.

Dr. Aponte ushers us in, not seeming taken aback by our unusual conveyance. He examines Felipe's left breast with its sore eruption and shakes his head. "There's nothing I can do," he says. "She needs pain medicine."

He advises us to buy morphine, tells us there's no prescription needed.

We get Felipe back in the truck. I go to the *farmacia* in town while Lexi keeps watch.

When I return, I see Lexi has bought Felipe an ice cream cone. Felipe is smiling wanly, licking at it a little. I've discovered it is possible to buy morphine without a prescription. I have a thermos of water and help Felipe take one of the pills. When we bring her home to her daughters, I go over the pill schedule carefully with them, counting out how many pills, and explain when to give them.

After I have more time and experience in the community, I will learn where to take patients to get chemotherapy or radiation. But I'm new to it all today and can only trust the doctor's opinion, and at least we get Felipe out of pain.

My kids, Rod and Trish, and friends at Maryknoll Sending Ceremony.

Photos

Aymara women welcome us in traditional ceremony.

Our first home next door to the established missioners.

A village scene, women threshing

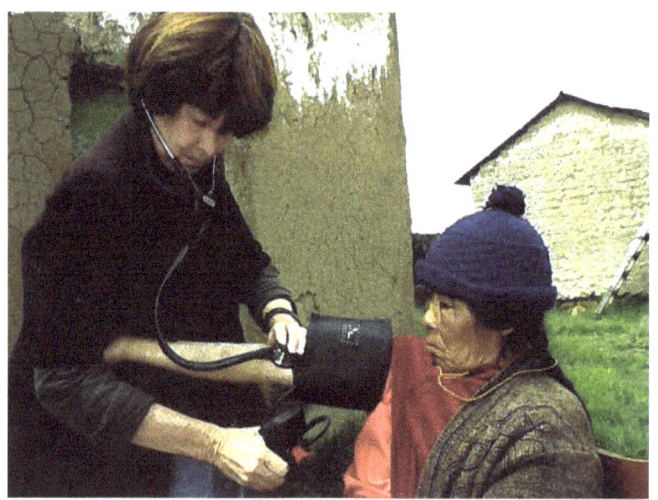

Seeing patients at Suzanne's clinic

Photos

Sister Francie, with Lexi top, Lucy bottom, long established with her nuns in Peru, finds us homes.

My home for the three years in Peru, just a field away from Sister Francie & her sisters.

My landlady, Gabina

My neighbors Rene and his father and Ernesto getting ready to build me a fireplace.

Photos

Fun times too: Mary Kate (front left), me, Lucy, (front right), Lexi to my right, on a trip with other Maryknoll missioners.

After Lexi and Mary Kate leave, I take a trip to Arequipa with Vicente and Rufina to get her needed quality care.

Neighborhood kids on the path outside my house, demonstrating their new toothbrushes.

A little boy who lost his hearing after an ear infection. His parents and I tried to find a way to help.

Photos

My kids, Jack and Jane, visit me in Peru, including a bus trip to Machu Picchu.

My neighbor Rene, and family accompanying, pack up and transport my furniture to storage for the next missioners.

Chapter 12
Village Life

OVER THE NEXT MONTHS, Lexi thinks she's found a place to rent. It's a big house in the cathedral town she favors. The house has an indoor bathroom with a shower. Sister Francie has continued to help both of us check out housing finds.

I love visiting Sister Francie and her convent of nuns in their little village of Camacani, which is much closer to Puno than Derek and Suzanne's outlying village, where Lexi and I are still living.

The sisters' place has a yard with flowers, a homey living room, a chapel. There is also a huge *carpa*, a green house made of thick plastic sheets over curved aluminum poles, capturing the hot sun so close to the Equator. I duck inside when I visit for a chance to feel warm. I love seeing the rows of broccoli and spinach and inhaling *summer*!

One day I'm there, Sister Francie says, "Take a walk with me."

We go the long way around, down to the road and back up the lane, not to walk on the planted field that divides the convent house from her neighbor's. Gabina, the neighbor, is an older widow living on her own who would consider renting me three of her rooms, Sister tells me.

As we walk up the rutted lane to the property, I see four small adobe dwellings around a hard-packed mud yard. There's a fence in front made of the same adobe mud blocks with a rough wooden gate marking the entrance. Each dwelling has a picturesque, thatched roof. I am charmed; it's old Ireland! I tell Sister it's just what I want.

She looks at me squarely. "Do you like mice and bugs?" Now I'm listening.

We stand and survey the property. I'm more realistic now. I learn that Gabina herself lives in the good-sized rectangular room along the left side. Along the back is another big room, up a few adobe steps. We walk into the yard. No sign of Gabina, but she's given us permission to look through. When I peer into the building on the right, I see it's actually two attached rooms. I quickly calculate: a living room/kitchen in the good-sized back room, a bedroom in the little back section of the building on the right, and a nice big room for a clinic just inside the gate with a bench by its door. Perfect!

In the next week, we strike a deal and give the men in the village a lot of work: changing the roofs to corrugated aluminum and replacing the charming wooden doors with steel ones. The water is supplied by a pump in the yard that spills into a low concrete basin about the size of a bathtub.

The men repair the outhouse, which is a few steps outside the front gate, adding the window I ask for, a request the workers evidently find hilarious. I add candles and a little mug with flowers.

More than once as I'm getting established in my new home, I come upon women peeking in all my windows.

"They're just curious," one of the fathers tells me. "They've never seen the like."

When it's complete, Lexi visits and says she likes it all and gives my outhouse the Good Housekeeping Seal of Approval: "It doesn't smell."

Lexi settles on her house too. The two of us have spent days riding around in Sister Francie's jeep, walking up and down dusty roads together in search of housing. Lexi likes the house in Chuquito, a town even closer to Puno than my choice. Chuquito has an ancient cathedral and a big plaza. Its streets, more like winding pathways, are filled with beautifully colored mosaic designs - stylized birds and native plants - worked into the concrete. Mostly the town consists of humble houses and a couple of little stores. The group of women already meeting there weekly make sweaters of alpaca to sell in the local markets. Lexi thinks she can help them work up to an export trade.

The pastor of Chuquito also shows Lexi a house in a nearby village. Later, as is protocol, she has an interview with him to say she wants to live and work in his parish.

"And do you prefer the city or the country house?" he asks, referring to the two sites he's shown her. Lexi, steeped in Manhattan life, asks earnestly, "Which one is the city?"

Once she settles on the big house in Chuquito, she needs to inform Suzanne and Derek. We go to Puno to call them in the US, where they're on annual leave. I'm standing by the phone for moral support. Rents are typically about ninety soles a month, $30 US. The doctor's house Lexi is thinking of renting costs $100 a month US, so maybe, on principle, not acceptable. In the telephone corner of the center's living room, Lexi rehearses her approach, interrupted by us breaking up laughing. But somehow, she presents the rental figure to Suzanne and it's a go.

After Lexi moves to Chuquito, we keep the jeep in her big, fenced yard or at my place.

At first, I park it outside my house on the rutted road, just alongside the outhouse. But more than once, all my neighbors, men and women, help me get it out of the mud with planks and ropes. This is when I learn that the Aymara people never give up on anything. After a few episodes of the people shouting instructions to each other and wet clumps of dirt flying everywhere, Sister Francie offers me their convent yard, just across the field from my house. It has a big fence and a gate. I'm to yell for one of the sisters to come unlock the gate and they'll let me in.

When Suzanne and Derek are back from leave, I drive out to work with Suzanne at her weekly clinic. I so appreciate this. We see and treat a lot of folks with high blood pressure, diabetes, arthritis, and coughs and colds. It's a much-needed orientation for working with the Aymara people on my own.

· · · · ·

After several months, when Lexi and I are fully settled into our own places, Suzanne and Derek are due to leave Peru for good, their mission commitment complete. Before they leave, the couple invites me for a picnic at a protected little beach on the lake. There, the three of us, sitting snug on blankets, have a talk. They make a case for me to move to their village and take over the clinic. I decline. I want a daily clinic. My new home is closer to Puno and closer to the nuns next store and Sister Marie down the hill and closer to Lexi. Suzanne and Derek's home is a good half hour from Puno and removed from all the people I've grown close to and appreciate.

And I am acclimating to life in my village. I cook and boil water for drinking on my two- burner propane stove, get washed in my room out of an enamel pan. It becomes routine. With delight I hang a sign in my clinic window, *La Clinica de Las Cordilleras*, The Clinic of the High Mountains, and soon I have patients every day.

I post clinic hours: 8 a.m. to noon, weekdays. Lexi and Sister Aurelia and Sister Maria, the two Maryknoll nuns we are closest to, tease me about this. The sisters, old hands in Peru, know the people well. They predict exactly how it will go. The folks will come much earlier, on their way to gather reeds along the lake to feed their animals. I'm up early, but often I see patients at the gate while I'm having coffee at 6 a.m.

Early on I try negotiating, "Come to the clinic on your way back up."

But I learn that I won't see them again that day as they have to feed the animals and tend their fields. So having let go of my idea, I wind up with plenty of patients, early and late.

A lot of people come with sore hands. It is always cold here, and their knuckles grow sore and swollen from pulling reeds from the cold lake. They have colds and sinus infections and sometimes troubling coughs. I have to unwrap layers of sweaters and lengths of wool to listen to their chests. I learn where to take patients for X-rays and lab work. One wife comes asking for socks for her husband. Most people here don't wear socks. They wear rubber tire sandals. Her husband's feet are cold. Mine would be too without my thick wool socks and sturdy boots. I find him socks at a booth that caters to tourists in the street market.

I'm filling my new bookcase with medical charts. My neighbor, Rene, made the bookcase. He makes simple furniture for his wife to sell at the Puno market. Rene and Patricia live just up the hill from me with their two young sons. I see the boys out flying kites in the hills above us in late afternoon after school, when the shadow of the mountains makes for early dusk.

One patient, a woman, describes her symptoms, and it sounds like diabetes. If so, she will need medicine for the rest of her life. Sure enough, the lab confirms diabetes. I buy enough pills to get her started, and I'm eager to see if she feels better. At the next visit she says she took all the pills and thanks me for curing her. I have a lot to learn.

People often knock at my gate and ask if I will come see someone in the family. One woman comes and tells me her husband is in pain when he walks and is starting to stay in bed a lot of the time. She draws me a map to their home. The next day I drive there and pull into their yard, planning to get him to the hospital in Puno for an X-ray. Her husband, Silva, about fifty years old, is in bed, dressed in a suit including a hat - not an Aymara knit cap but a Stetson. He reminds me of my father. We get him up, and with his makeshift crutch we slowly make our way out to the Land Rover across their stony yard.

The hospital in Puno is a large, unheated, concrete building, colder inside than out. As we walk down the corridor, I see patients fully dressed in warm sweaters and wool caps in their hospital beds. X-ray films show that Silva has a bad case of arthritis —no fracture. We stop at the pharmacy and get him a good supply of ibuprofen. I warn him to take it with food. I draw him stick figure exercises of simple stretches to do every day.

As the days go by, I often see Sister Marie next door at Sister Francie's when I'm invited for evening prayer. In a simply decorated room with the nuns gathered around a low table for an altar, someone reads; we all respond. Among the sisters I feel peace.

Village Life

After one of these evenings, Sister Marie and I walk back to our homes together. Before we part, Marie asks me if I want to do home visits with her the next day. I haven't felt familiar enough with the nearby villages to have done that on my own, so I'm glad for the offer.

With her the next day I see the poorest of the poor who I have yet to see in Peru. We visit an old man. He's in trousers and a faded shirt, his gray hair limp. He's not fretting, just very still. Lying on a doubled-up blanket in a one-room adobe dwelling that we have to crawl into, he acknowledges us with his eyes and a feeble flicker of his hand. Sister Marie unwraps the pills she's brought and asks if he has water. In the dim light he points to a tin cup in a little niche dug out of the rounded adobe wall. This is his home. He is without family. She helps him take the medicine she brings him on a regular basis, leaves him more water, and tells him she'll see him again soon.

In the Altiplano, the high plains, she tells me as we walk back, the adult children often go off to find work in the cities. In many cases, the elderly are left alone for months at a time, dependent on the contributions of their family or their own meager earnings from farming or market sales. Many a robust older person packs up produce or wares and takes the jitney to Puno, spending the day earning a few soles. A sickly older person suffers.

One Sunday, not long after, the women in my village are sitting out in the sun on a slight rise of ground near me, smiling and chatting, glad to be free of fieldwork for the day.

I join them. With their legs straight out in front of them, their thick layers of felt skirts tucked around them, they beam contentment. Several are weaving strands of alpaca into thread on heavy wooden spools. The conversation takes a typical turn, how is it in the United States? What is it like?

They want to talk about - in their and my basic Spanish- how could I leave my fields.

How I got here. They talk too about their children needing to move away from the village to find work. Several are middle-aged women, some with young children, still capable of farming or selling at the market.

But an older woman, her brown face lined and cracked like dry soil, talks about how hard it is when you can't work like you could before. I tell her about Social Security. She looks astonished.

"The government sends you money?" "Yes."

I explain how you earn money all the years on your job and the government takes money out of your pay for many years. She looks out over the fields, then looks at me with a big smile.

"Tell me again about that Social Security," she says softly.

Chapter 13
No Sheep

A FEW WEEKS after that enjoyable Sunday, I head into town for medical supplies. I board a very full jitney bus, climbing over people and their bulky bundles and flapping chickens to find a little seat at the very back.

"Boy! You have to be an acrobat to ride this bus!"

And they all start laughing, me with them. At that moment I feel very much a part of the community.

That I have access to a vehicle at least some of the time is very popular with my neighbors. Otherwise, a trip to Puno for them entails carrying market goods or heavy baskets of food down our rutted path to catch a jitney. Rene hefts his handmade benches and stools down the hill for his wife, Patricia, hoping it's not too long before one of the little buses comes along to take her to market. I've seen grandmothers come along with heavy metal trays packed with potatoes, helped by a son or neighbor. The woman knows that once she gets to the bus, the bus workers will lift her heavy goods, or if furniture, tie it down on the roof. There is an Aymara concept, called *annai*, that is about you being there for your neighbor when they need help, and that you can expect the same in return.

Today, Rene asks me to drive him up higher into the mountains as his mother has taken sick up there and needs to go to the hospital. Along with Patricia and their two school-age sons, the kite flyers, their household includes his mother and father. Periodically, the old couple brings a herd of sheep up into the mountains for more pasture.

I don't know how Rene got word about his mother being sick up there, but he needs my help to bring her down. One of the Maryknoll priests had told me once about their sixth sense. "You may not see them, but they are always aware of what you are doing."

We walk through a few scattered sheep droppings, like hard raisins, to get the Land Rover from Sister Francie's yard. I know how to open the gate by now. One of the sisters, heading for the *carpa*, waves and says she'll close it.

Ernesto, another neighbor, comes up to the jeep while we're getting settled and asks to come along. Then Rene's wife comes running with their boys.

Okay, we can manage, I think. Rene in front with me as my guide; Ernesto and Patricia on the back bench seats with the boys. Then Ernesto's wife comes along, juggling a sheep in her arms.

"Can you take it?"

"No, no sheep!" I apologize to them, "I have to draw the line at sheep."

Good thing too, because once we are high up in the trackless mountains, I am feeling totally lost and frazzled.

"Rene, I can't go much farther," I say after endless ups and downs over rounded swells of grass and dirt. He assures me we are almost there, as he has been saying for the past half hour. Finally, coming around a bend, I see a little wooden dwelling with his parents sitting side by side on a bench outside. It's chilly up here, and we are glad for our warm jackets, but the glorious view of the

No Sheep

snowcapped blue mountains and the endless expanse of sky is our reward.

We assure Rene's father that I'll take his wife to the hospital. She seems to be straining to breathe. He will stay up here with the sheep. I did not think to bring food, but these are the people who stay out in the fields on winter nights in makeshift huts to keep putting water over small potatoes, making them into what they call *chuño*. *Chuño* stays edible through the season when people can't grow potatoes and quinoa, their mainstays. I've nibbled at it, found it a testament to the people's fortitude.

With the mother comfortable in a warm shawl, the kids sitting cross-legged on the floor below the adults, we are ready to go back down the mountain. As I start the engine, I think I hear Rene conferring with his father, who wants him to take one sheep back with us. Rene seems to be explaining the no-sheep rule.

As we near Puno, Rene says they'll take the jitney home so I can get his mother straight to the hospital. There, a doctor diagnoses a heart problem, not urgent, and he gives her medicine and an appointment to come back in a week.

When I'm driving back into town with Rene's mother for the follow-up appointment, with several neighbors catching a ride, we are stopped, to my surprise, by a policeman. There is a new law, he's telling me, I'm guessing promoted by the jitney drivers, that you cannot pick up people waiting for the bus and drive them into town. It looks like I have done just that.

I take a moment, then say, "They're my family."

He gives me a stern look, then his face softens, and he waves us on.

Chapter 14

Miracles and Misery

WELL INTO THE first year, I'm looking over the fields from my kitchen window, glad for quiet before the first farmer knocks. Then I hear shouting and banging on the gate, more urgent than usual. I cross the yard quickly. Rene has made me big, flat steppingstones, hacked one afternoon out of a nearby big rock. I open the gate to see a young couple standing there. She's dressed in the thick felt skirts of the Aymara women and is pregnant and in pain. She's holding fast to her husband's hand.

"*Hermana*, Sister, can you take us? My wife is going to have the baby."

"Wait right here," I say. I already have my jacket on from the cold kitchen and head across the field of quinoa, carefully jumping between the rows, to get the jeep from the nuns' yard.

I'm praying, *Let the jeep start.* The rock and nail are on hand, but it starts on its own. I quickly drive back to my house and help them down the rough path to the paved road and into the jeep. The young woman's groans grow louder as we speed along the road. Her husband is giving me directions and says her name, Ascencia. "My wife is Ascencia."

Let me remember how to help her give birth, I pray, *better yet, get us there.*

Down the road we fly. Her husband spots the place, a small building with a clinic sign painted on the outside. Between us, we help Ascencia into the building; She is barely able to walk.

Inside, two young women, the midwives, take over calmly, with assurance and smiles.

They guide Ascencia onto to a gurney and position themselves to assist her. In the plain concrete room, the midwives have a gurney with a paper sheet over it, squares of gauze, and a basin with soap and water. Not much else.

Then the baby is pushing out. The midwives are kind and gentle, soothing the mother and alert to catch the baby. With crying all around —the baby girl, the new mother, and me —it is accomplished. Tears of joy. I am so relieved.

The young couple are going to stay the night at the clinic. I say I'll come back and take them home the next day. I thank the beautiful young midwives. "You are angels," I tell them. I drive home counting my blessings for their competence, their goodness.

· · · · ·

About a week later, I want to visit the new mother and the baby. One of my villagers tells me she is staying with her parents. He gives me directions and a helpful kilometer marker.

I am pleased to find it. It's an adobe house with a sloping stretch of land in front. A low wall of stones surrounds the property by the road where I park. I tuck the Land Rover onto a patch of grass and head up the hill to the house.

The custom for visiting someone here is to stand outside where you can be seen and shout to make your presence known.

When I am almost to the house I see the two dogs, who start barking wildly and running toward me. Running and stumbling, I drop my backpack. As I scoop it up one dog bites me in the calf, and I feel a second bite a little lower in the other leg.

I drive straight to the clinic in town, dreading that I might need a series of rabies needles in my stomach. I am angry as I bump along in the jeep, but once I get there, the young attendant, Carlos, is welcoming and reassuring. He cleans the wounds, smearing on antiseptic. My jeans have prevented one bite from breaking the skin, but the skin is pierced on the other leg.

Carlos says he'll check with the family to see if the dogs have been given rabies shots. Rabies inoculation is standard throughout the district, he tells me. He is going to go right then, and I say I'll follow in the jeep. It's comforting to remind myself as I ride along that I received a prophylactic rabies injection and booster at the end of Maryknoll's mission training. When we get back to the house, the girl's mother comes out. Not only is she not apologetic, but she is shouting angrily at me. For trespassing, I guess.

The Aymara people can seem cold and distrustful, unlike the warm, effusive Central Americans I'd known from previous mission trips. But the Aymara people's distrust of whites may come from a history of being duped out of their land by the authorities. This explains their retreat to land at such high altitudes, land deemed undesirable by their oppressors. Or maybe the mother is just mad at me for interfering with her family, from her point of view.

But the dogs had their shots. Carlos could verify. My ride home is peaceful. The fields of potatoes slip by, smelling of rich, fresh dirt. The beautiful mountains loom in the distance, and the car started with only one solid whack.

Chapter 15
Hard Times

MONTHS ROLL BY, filled with routine clinic days, and getting to know my Aymara neighbors and other missioners. Then, a year in, a nice change. We are getting a third missioner, Mary Kate. I'm driving along Lake Titicaca to pick up Lexi. We'll stay overnight at the Center House and tomorrow take a taxi to the airport for the trip to Lima, where we'll meet her. I'm enjoying the break in routine. I spot Lexi ahead and pull up to our designated meeting spot.

"Do you know we've been here one year?" I say in greeting.

She climbs into the Land Rover's faded leather seat beside me and checks the glovebox. "Yep, and we now know how to start a battery with a rock and a nail, something that will surely come in handy back in civilization."

Chuckling, I start driving. Like today's plan, we have stayed at the Maryknoll Center in Puno many weekends before. There's no heat in the building, which is true everywhere in the Altiplano, but the showers have hot water. To use it, I bring all my clean clothes in with me, including underwear, turtleneck shirt, thick sweater, fleece vest and wool socks, and boots. I dry and dress quickly afterward before the cold from the concrete floor seeps through. It is also the house bathroom, so no lingering.

The weather is chilly with an overcast sky as Lexi and I arrive at the center. We haul laundry and overnight bags across the large cement parking lot inside the gates. In South America's upside-down climate, this month, July, is winter. December is as close to balmy as it gets in the Altiplano.

As we gather our clothes to wash in the open shed off the yard, I ask Lexi, "Do you think it could snow? Should we hang them inside?" "Nah, it never snows here."

That afternoon, looking out at the clothesline with our pajamas and sweatshirts draped in snow, we chortle and take pictures of it outside in the yard with the house cooks, two great guys who put up with us occasionally invading their kitchen.

Over coffee in the big living room, after we've hung our clothes to dry in our rooms, our conversation turns serious. I am talking about my work at my clinic. I have patients most mornings. In early afternoon, I do house chores or home visits. Sometimes I need a trip to the pharmacy or the lab in town. I take the jeep if I have it, or I walk down the village path to the highway and wait for the jitney.

I am learning the people's ways. I tell Lexi that in the clinic, the women offer me potatoes as payment, held up in their aprons, so as not to touch my hands, I guess. I try to convince them, one, that we are two equal women, and they can hand them to me. And two, that I have to pay for the medicine in soles at the pharmacy. I can't pay in potatoes. Plus, I am one person. I point to the sack of potatoes in the corner and say, "How many potatoes do you think I can eat?" They laugh.

But Lexi is having a different experience. She's struggling.

"Too much downtime," she says. "The women's co-op doesn't meet every day. The women don't understand the idea of designing goods for the US market. One batch of men's sweaters had llamas and roses decorating the front."

She pulls a sample out of a bag. It's a confusing mix of color and design. I roll my eyes.

Lexi's home in the grand house she rents from the Puno doctor is some compensation for her. It's gracious and luxurious by Altiplano standards with a big, gated garden and a patio. It has a second floor, with her *Princess* bedroom, as I call it, and a real bathroom with a toilet, sink, and shower on the first floor.

She is also using her financial skills to help the bishop write a grant. Lexi was vice president of the Financial Resources Department at Columbia. In her local grant effort, she often drives back and forth to the bishop's residence in his town of Juli, a long ride from her town, even out beyond Suzanne and Derek's village. But, overall, she is becoming disenchanted.

"What was I thinking?" she says, laughing.

Her riding back and forth to help the bishop turns out to prove the depth of our friendship. One night I am staying over at her house in one of the bedrooms on the first floor. She is so late in returning, I lock the large creaky gate, feeling a little scared alone in her big house. I think she must be staying overnight at the bishop's residence. His big house has multiple dorm-type rooms for the seminarians (priests-to-be) who live there and also for guests.

But she returns later in a hard rain, finds the gate locked, and must walk back down the hill and wrestle with another gate, where she parked the car, and then drive the jeep into Puno. The next day when I hear her at the gate, thinking she is just getting home from the bishop's, I tease her, "Are you having an affair with the bishop?"

When she explains what happened, I feel terrible, apologizing profusely, but Lexi is gracious, and it becomes one more running joke. And it lets me know what a forgiving bond we have forged between us.

And she throws great dinner parties in her big house. The fathers and sisters love to come and sit around her table in the big dining/sitting area. The house has concrete floors and walls, but Lexi makes it charming with art and candles and the Inca-patterned rugs sold in every market stall. She even has a fireplace, built by my neighbor Rene and his father. Her house has become a great meeting place.

One Sunday, one of the young fathers conducts a Mass for a small group of us there.

Afterward we sit around the fireplace, warm and happy, chatting away. I point all this out to her as we sit looking out at the snow-covered yard. She smiles and sighs but doesn't say anything further.

We start talking about our trip to Lima to welcome Mary Kate. We'll bring her back to Puno with us. We know this much about her: she's had previous mission experience in Central America, has been a high school religion teacher, and is thirty-four years old. We now have all the decades covered.

We're up early the next day and on our way to the airport. Getting to Lima is always a thrill for us. For one, it's considerably warmer at sea level on the Pacific seacoast. In warm weather, we'd eat out on the patio of our favorite Italian restaurant, walkable from the Lima Center, a jumping-for-joy luxury. Though it's winter now, we'll certainly take Mary Kate to eat inside the restaurant during our interval in Lima. I will always remember the name of the red wine I savor there, Alto Las Hormigas. Above the Ants! Despite its odd name, it's rich and delicious.

When Mary Kate comes through the door in Lima that evening, she impresses as clear- spoken, friendly and fun. She's young with short hair, wearing a practical vest and jeans. That first evening I think we all know we will be comfortable sharing the same fun and ease that Lexi and I enjoy.

Then we discover that Derek is already in Lima. He says he is planning to take Mary Kate by bus over the border to La Paz, Bolivia, for an overnight orientation. Once she returns to Lima, we'll bring her to Lexi's house, where she'll stay until she finds work and a place to live.

Going over the border to La Paz is a trial by fire, or so Derek made it seem when Lexi and I first went over with him. In his style, he gave us a lot of details about safety and the crossing procedure. In actuality, it's a bus ride from Puno and a walk through the border crossing station to have passports checked (and stored on the Peru side), then a walk to board the same bus now waiting just on the other side in Bolivia. To be fair to Derek, on one crowded walk across the boundary, I had my wallet swiped out of my bag. My bag was so jammed full it was gaping open, so it was my carelessness entirely. I should have listened to the pickpocketing talk.

Derek and Mary Kate will stay over in the Maryknoll Center House in La Paz. That house is at an even higher altitude than where we live. The surrounding mountains are beautiful and always snowcapped. When we go there for regional meetings, the streets are so steep leading up to the big house that we arrive at the front door puffing and panting, nearly collapsing inside the foyer. We call it the Ice Palace. I've heard a rumor that it was once occupied by Nazis or maybe had been the German Embassy. It certainly is grand, with a wide two-story staircase leading up to the nicely appointed chilly rooms upstairs.

But we still have a full day with Mary Kate in Lima before her trip, so next morning the three of us take a walk to the ocean to show her the people taking running leaps off the cliff and kite-sailing over the ocean. A little further up the coast, we go to the little park with beautifully colored mosaics worked into all the bordering rocks. We sit and enjoy them, pointing out the sayings and symbols to each other. Lima, unfortunately, for all its cosmopolitan feel, is perpetually overcast. "Pizarro's Revenge," they call it. No sun, ever. We take Mary Kate to our favorite downtown restaurant, reached by walking along the wide, tree-lined boulevard.

"You two walk too fast!" Mary Kate lets us know.

With its outdoor terrace, surrounded by a trimmed privacy hedge and space heaters, it is a luxury. Most importantly, we want time to give Mary Kate a little preparation for Derek, who has scheduled them for an early bus to La Paz the next day. We savor our café con leches and share our experiences and impressions of Derek.

We say things like, "You may have a different experience with him," and "He's trying to be helpful." Somehow, through it all, we are laughing. When we get hungry, Lexi and I order salads.

"Words you will never hear pass my lips," Mary Kate says as she orders a burger.

We're up early the next morning to see them off. We give Mary Kate and Derek hugs and wish them a good trip as they scramble out the door to their waiting taxi, which is a regular car, driven by the son of one of the cooks, a typical arrangement.

"He's basically a good guy," we say to each other as we walk back in. We had made that point to Mary Kate, reassuring ourselves that we hadn't gone overboard in advising her. We agree, he just seems to get caught up in his role as the experienced missionary, the one with all the knowledge. Mary Kate impresses me as quite capable of asserting herself with him.

Later that day, when Lexi and I are in line to have dinner in the center's dining room, a couple of the fathers who live there ask if we heard about the trouble Derek and the new missioner had crossing the border. Just then I see Derek across the dining room, standing chatting with a few of the priests at one of the tables.

Then Mary Kate enters the room and rapidly crosses over to us. "I can't eat," she says, "I just wanted to find you."

"Let's go up to one of our rooms."

She sits at my desk, looking pale and tense.

"It was horrible," she says, "We were shot at."

"What?! What happened?" Lexi gets up and puts her arm around her.

"We were on the bus. Then all of a sudden, it stopped. Bolivian people on strike had piled big stones on the road. Then we heard shouts and looked up toward the hills. All these soldiers came over the top shooting guns. The people on the road started throwing rocks. The women on the bus covered the windows with their shawls and blankets. I turned to look at Derek, like "What do we do?"

But he was going down the stairs of the bus and out the door. "I was by myself, so scared ...not knowing."

She starts to cry, and we both hug her, hold her. She just shakes her head slowly, tears falling. I picture Derek as I had just seen him, relaxed and chatting.

I say, "He seems so nonchalant just now."

"He's making light of it," Mary Kate says, "He didn't apologize or explain on the way home. He said it's a typical mission experience."

We help her with her coat and go outside.

"Let's go get pizza," Lexi says. "There's a place a block away."

As we come out of the restaurant, I reach up behind Mary Kate and pass her hat over her shoulder. She had forgotten it in the booth. She jumps about a foot. We kind of laugh, all of us, but also Lexi and I are looking at her closely, seeing that she has been truly shaken to the core, our new friend, clear-spoken, assertive Mary Kate.

Mary Kate's anxiety persists. Like most new missioners arriving at their new site, she has no established home and no sense of what her work will be. Her sense of unease is doubled. It's the beginning of months of painful anxiety for her, punctuated at times, ironically, by some of our happiest days. Mary Kate is staying at Lexi's. When I can, I stay there overnight too.

Hanging wash in the garden, preparing dinner together for the priests and nuns, or just ourselves, cleaning up afterward, sometimes close to midnight, I love the sense of warmth and trust we share. One time I mess up on something, then Lexi forgets a message she was supposed to pass on.

"Between the three of us," I say, "we make one good missioner." And that becomes our motto and our best bonding joke.

Chapter 16
One Third Missioners

"**THE THREE OF US** make one good missioner," we often laugh and say, as we settle into our communities and get working on projects, but it is far from perfect. Mary Kate is struggling with a new missionary's first-year dilemma of finding a work niche, and Lexi continues to find her Women's Cooperative meetings too infrequent. As often as we can, we stay at the Center House in Puno on weekends. For me, depending on who has the Land Rover, its just a short drive along Lake Titicaca, or catching a jitney ride.

Mary Kate has settled much farther out, so she can only join us when her housemates, Sister Maria and Sister Aurelia, are driving in. We're looking forward to seeing Mary Kate and the sisters this weekend.

I'm driving today and point to the foothills clustered around the crossroads that enter Puno then sweep up into the high Andes. We often forget we're at high altitude, but climbing a flight of outdoors stairs, like those to the cathedral office, I feel short of breath and think, *wow, I'm getting old!* Then I remember.

"I love the way the mountains are always changing colors," I say. Lexi smiles, nodding. The whole landscape is different for us and can be startlingly beautiful. Entering Puno, though, the outskirts hold the town dump. We stop discreetly alongside as I snap a photo of an Aymara woman and her little girl rummaging in the mounds of trash, raising sulfurous dust.

Beyond the dump is a plain wide street with rebar rods sticking up on many of the flat-roofed houses, awaiting second floors. This is the newer section.

Further along is the old city We pass the high cyclone fence around the hospital yard and see the guard admitting visitors through the gate. Next is the ancient railroad station, appearing huddled into itself, with a low-sloped roof. It offers trips to Machu Picchu that can take eleven hours. The bus, boarded at the more modern depot on the outskirts of town, takes four to five.

Parked safely inside the gate at the Center House, we meet up with Mary Kate and walk together up the wide cobblestone street to the open-air shopping area. We'll see the sisters later at dinner. Aymara ladies sit under draped plastic shelters displaying their wares on beautifully woven blankets. The women, with their long, thick braids and several layers of wool skirts and derby hats, are always happily chatting with each other. We learn early on that the women do not want their pictures taken. They make stern faces, wagging their fingers at us and turning away.

Further up the wide walkway, off-limits to cars, small shops display tourist treasures. We look at the pottery and beautiful alpaca sweaters, pointing out our favorites to each other. At one corner is an attractive little hotel with only a closet-sized lobby featuring a steep, winding stairway to the rooms above. Mary Kate slips in and goes up to see what is above the street view.

"A small hall with a few doors off of it," she reports, "not the Hilton."

One Third Missioners

We pass a pizza shop we enjoy featuring a wood-fired oven. Our favorite stop, a little further up, is the town's only coffee shop. There we sit and order delicious café con leches.

Mary Kate is feeling frustrated.

"The sisters have great projects going. So far, I just follow them around. I wish Maryknoll had set us up with a project."

"It took us a long time too," Lexi says.

"Lucy could jump into medicine, but I'm having a hard time getting the women to design their sweaters for the US market, which is how I think I can best help them. One woman brought in a man's sweater with llamas and roses on the front. I showed Lucy."

"Oh! too funny," Mary Kate laughs. "I can imagine the look on a man's face who receives one as a Christmas present."

We all laugh and finish our coffee, scraping back our chairs on the aged black and white tiled floor. We wave goodbye to the now familiar owner, standing by his prized copper cappuccino machine, and head for the big indoor market to buy food.

The market is a huge, tin-roofed place, with rows and rows of vendors' stalls piled high with potatoes and vegetables, fish and chicken. It's chilly and the concrete floor is slippery as I make my way to my favorite young mother and little boy from whom I regularly buy spinach and other dark greens for pennies.

"You should charge more," I tell the mother. She just smiles; her little boy looks up solemnly with dark, luminous eyes. Lexi and Mary Kate are off on their own purchases, and as usual we'll meet back at the Center House and all have supper there.

In the midst of this comfortable routine, I puzzle from time to time over the occasional hints I've heard of Peru's recent darker history, the time of *Sendera Luminosa*, The Shining Path.

Many of the nuns and priests still stationed here lived through it, but they rarely talk about it. Nor do the villagers in my community. The Shining Path, I read and gleaned from a few remarks, was active for about eight years until 1996 when the leader, Abmael Guzman, a college professor turned anarchist, was captured. Lexi and I came five years after that.

Once, on a group excursion into foothills country, an isolated area with soft rolling planes and strong winds that bowed down the long grass, Lexi, Mary Kate, and I were shown a building that had been bombed by Sendera insurgents. It had housed a program founded by a Peruvian organization for women, called "A Cup of Milk a Day." One woman was killed in the bombing. A beautiful young woman, her portrait was displayed in the restored building. I was astonished.

"Who could be against milk for children?" I asked the people who had guided us to the site. I just didn't understand what *Sendera Luminosa* had been about. I've been able to learn more from staying at the Center House talking to the nuns and priests. I am often in Puno to buy medicine or drop something off at the lab, and if it grows late and too dark to navigate the road home along the lake, I stay over in one of the little rooms available to us.

Some evenings I talk with Sister Pat, one of my favorites, an experienced Maryknoll nun whose calm self-assurance always inspires me. After Sister Pat's first stint in Peru, she served in the Maryknoll sisters' governing council of five. When that commitment was completed, as the nuns regularly rotate leadership, Sister Pat returned to Puno. Now, during my time, she is working as a paralegal in a Puno law office.

After dinner sometimes, Sister Pat and I talk in the big living room, next to the library, my treasure house. The room full of books also houses a TV, very popular with everybody in the house at news time, though I struggle with it being in Spanish, which of course it is.

Talking with Sister Pat is the real opening to my understanding of The Shining Path. In her current role as a paralegal, Sister Pat settles neighbors' water rights feuds, inheritance conflicts, marital disputes, and the like. As she talks in the abstract about the cases, I admire her commonsense approach to restoring justice and relationships.

She says the bombing of the Cup of Milk project grew out of Sendera's Marxist philosophy. They saw society as hopelessly corrupt and that it needed to be destroyed, leveled to the ground, and a new society built in its place.

"When Sendera was active," Sister Pat says, "I tried to help parents whose sons or daughters were missing, presumably forced into service with the revolutionary army. The lines weren't clear between the regular army and the hundreds of young men and women recruited by Guzman, the founder. Guzman had them sign a loyalty oath, not to the country or even to Sendera, but to himself. He called himself *Presidente* Guzman."

"Right here in Puno, there was an army barracks and the *comandante* had his office here. I used to visit him on a regular basis. I wanted to find out if the young people the parents were searching for were in there or if the comandante would at least tell me if he knew they'd been conscripted. I kept trying to get information any way I could. I came week after week."

"I made a little headway when I told him, "'I come to you, Comandante, because I know you are a man who knows the law. You know that parents must be informed if their children are under the army's jurisdiction.'"

"Flattery seemed to get through to him," she says, laughing. "When I came back the next week and was coming down the hall to his office, he greeted me heartily, "'Ah, Sister Relentless!'"

Sendera, she told me, had killed thousands of people before their reign ended. In their quest to dismantle existing leadership, such as mayors of villages, they'd kill the authorities, then conscript the young villagers for soldiers.

I learned more another weekend. Lexi invited Mary Kate and Sister Aurelia and Sister Maria to lunch at her big house before they set out on their long ride back to their remote village. I was always included and loved these laid-back, chatty times.

Sister Aurelia, born in the US of Mexican parents, was another favorite of mine. Tall and sensible, funny and warmhearted, she was an agronomist who worked a deal with the farmers. If they didn't use the genetically modified seeds from the big corporations, she'd provide regular seeds at an affordable price.

She made me laugh when she told me the kids in Camacani, where I now live, saw a group of nuns coming into the village and said, "Look, it's the Aurelias!"

Sister Maria, a Peruvian native, kind and gentle, offered people holistic medical treatments.

The two nuns were a wonderful pair, beloved by the people for their knowledge and their understanding of the Aymara culture. Mary Kate was happy to have found a home with them. She calls Pilcuyo, the town where they live, "the place where God goes for vacation."

That day over lunch, I prompted the sisters to share another Sendera story. Sister Maria told of driving one night on the main road to Camacani, being pursued at top speed, headlights flashing into her car. She careened into the little cow path that serves as the entry road to our village and screeched into the yard of the house, jumping out and pounding on the door, shouting out who she was. One of the Maryknollers, meeting there, pulled her inside and slammed and locked the door. Her pursuers surrounded the building, shouting and banging on the walls, eventually giving up.

Later that year, we get a taste of violence in our own time. We're in Puno when it erupts at the college in town. This makes people especially uneasy because Guzman, who started Sendera, was a college professor in Ayacucho, about 335 miles up the coast.

Mary Kate is an avid photographer and is eager to go into town and see it. Lexi is willing. I don't want to take the risk.

I say, drawing myself up in my superior age, "Girls, an out-of-control situation is out of control."

But off they go with me wringing my hands, watching as they start up the cobblestone street, Mary Kate's cameras dangling over her shoulders as she strides along with her characteristic gusto. Lexi leans in, listening.

I get a ride home that day with Sister Francie and a couple of her nuns from across my yard. I wind up staying with them all that afternoon. Our Aymara neighbors flock there, asking the sisters to use their phone, the only one in town, to call the local hospital to inquire about their sons and daughters who hadn't yet returned from town. Eventually all the young people return, telling tales of the army shooting in the air to quell the rioters. Lexi and Mary Kate swear they had stayed safely on the sidelines.

Toward the end of that year, Mary Kate mounts a collection of her beautiful photographs of the Aymara people all around the center's chapel walls. It beautifully enhances the atmosphere. She is a strong, gifted, independent woman, a Liturgist in her home church, and an appealing mix of no-nonsense practicality and deep-rooted creativity and lots of fun.

Another brush with violence occurs when the three of us pile into an old taxi, heading for the airport to pick up some visiting missioners. On the way, we must take several detours to avoid burning tires and, on one street, a burning car, torched as a strike protest.

We've been stopped at other times by villagers mounting strikes (*paros*), piling boulders on the road, stopping traffic to protest such ideas as privatization of water. Mary Kate knows all too well from her early experience that such situations can turn deadly.

Lexi and Mary Kate are watching closely, telling the driver in strained voices, "Be careful! No, don't go down that street!"

I'm trying to watch, but I'm preoccupied holding in the back window of the old cab that the driver pushed back into the frame just as we got in.

Chapter 17
A Surprise

BY THE THIRD YEAR, I've grown accustomed to my new life. I'm in the kitchen, limping a bit, favoring my ankle, boiling water, cleaning vegetables, giving myself a quiet day at home. The sun is splashing in on the little table and basin, my "sink." My place looks nice. As aways, I look out at the long view down to the main road and beyond to the distant glimmer of the lake.

Scrubbing away at a chunky potato, I'm remembering tripping yesterday as I came down the few rough stone steps from my living room/kitchen to the yard. I twisted my ankle. It hurt, I let out a loud groan. I wondered if Gabina, my Aymara landlady right across the yard, would hear me and come out. But no. I sat there a bit, then limped to my bedroom, dipped a cold cloth in my wash basin, wrung it out, and wrapped it around my ankle, then elevated it on a dry towel. Laying there, I pondered the differences in our cultures. In the US, a person would have run over and asked, "Are you all right?"

Or had Gabina not heard me? Or was she not wanting to embarrass me, seeing me sprawled out on the ground?

The difference in cultures can be hard. I'm usually comfortable reading people, but here sometimes, even with much better Spanish, I still sometimes feel puzzled, and they do too.

I've seen Gabina gathering leaves off our yard bushes for tea and later gifted her with a box of real tea. She was pleased. She then asked me about the flowers I grow in soup cans, "But what do they grow?" she said.

Thinking, I imagine of the quinoa grain that ripens after the plants glow red.

Years earlier, on a short mission trip to Oaxaca, Mexico, where I worked in a clinic, the nurse in charge told me to sit in front of the TV, like you would do to get a child out of your hair. She assumed I was dumb because at that time I couldn't communicate very well. During the clinic workday, the nurses would sometimes burst out laughing, sharing a joke I didn't get.

On that same trip to Oaxaca, I had helped an obstetrician birth a baby. *"¡Empuje! ¡Empuje!"* the doctor kept saying emphatically to the young mother. "'¡Push! ¡Push!"

· · · · ·

That same week the doctor invited me to go high into the hills with her to visit another new mother. This young woman had given birth on her own. Abandoned by her parents because she was not married, she had gone to a remote place and had the baby just that morning. Her brother had gotten word to the doctor.

We were driving up in an old car with the doctor's two young Mexican helpers doing the driving. Everybody was speaking Spanish. I caught some. Slowly we drove higher and higher with many jerks and starts up the winding dirt road. I was looking out the window, enjoying the view, when we got stuck.

A Surprise

We all piled out. Our back wheel was jammed in a deep rut. The doctor got the guys to go to the back of the car and said. *"¡Empuje, empuje!"* I started laughing.

"Doctor, *contigo es siempre! empuje! empuje!*" "With you it's always, push, push!"

And they all laughed, even the guys in spite of their strained, outstretched arms and faces grimacing as they pushed the car. My first joke in Spanish.

Up the beautiful Mexican hills we went that day, filled with trees and greenery in this part of the world. At the top we found a small, one-room frame house. Inside was a wooden bed and a makeshift kitchen of sorts. The doctor cleaned up the mother, a young woman with long, dark hair, brown beads of a rosary around her neck. When she was comfortable, I showed her the towels and diapers and milk, bread, and cheese that we had brought. As I showed her the new bars of soap in fresh wrappers, she looked at them with surprising joy. She was especially happy with these. That they were new, I think, and that we cared about her enough to bring the good stuff.

Before we left, I took the blanket from her bed outside to shake it, overlooking the valley and the hills we climbed. I felt joy, deep, quiet, and full.

· · · · ·

I'm smiling remembering all that, as I lay out the potatoes to dry in my own makeshift kitchen in Camacani. Such a gift, this opportunity. Then, to my surprise, I spot Lexi and Mary Kate coming toward the front gate, struggling to carry a big box between them.

I am delighted to see them. I knew they had gone to La Paz, but I didn't expect them.

"I'm surprised to see you!" I help them set the box on the bench outside the clinic. "Let's get this inside," Mary Kate says.

I make them instant coffee stirred into boiled milk, and we sit.

"Here's the thing," Lexi starts, and then she goes silent, her face looking worried. Mary Kate jumps in, "We're going to leave."

We all sit there frozen, me in astonished silence.

"You have the clinic," Lexi picks up, "and Mary Kate feels like she doesn't have anything meaningful to keep her here. And I feel the same."

"I'm coming to the end of finding this good for me," Lexi adds.

Mary Kate says, "You know I'm still a nervous wreck and angry. I'm sure it's PTSD, and taking the health leave at Maryknoll hasn't fixed it."

"I get it," I manage.

"So, we brought you a refrigerator," they chorus and start opening the box. It's a dorm-sized fridge, perfect for my little kitchen. The rest of the room serves as a living room. My neighbor Rene has made chairs and a table and even a bookcase with glass front doors, my nightly retreat.

I begin to muse. I have a year to go. I have the sisters next door and Maryknoll friends in town. I have a fireplace in my sitting space now, just like Lexi had our neighbor men construct in her house, a huge comfort in a house with no heat. And now I have a refrigerator, so I can buy chicken and vegetables for a week.

"I understand," I manage to get out. "I'm not going to fall apart, but I will miss you both so much."

A Surprise

"We feel terrible. I can't believe we're leaving you!" says Lexi.

Soon we hug and laugh. They have to rush back to Puno so Mary Kate can catch a ride with her two sister housemates to their remote home. I wave goodbye as they climb into the jeep and go back to scrubbing vegetables. I'm feeling a deep, extraordinary, unfathomable mood. I take deep breaths and reach for a bunch of carrots.

Once my dear pals are truly gone, my routine sustains me. As a fairly new physician assistant working solo, I can feel at the edge of my medical knowledge, but what the people typically present at the clinic I can handle. Arthritis, from foraging in cold Lake Titicaca, is common. Minor injuries, occasional diabetes and hypertension, that's my daily fare.

But about this time, Rufina, a young mother of five, presented to Sister Marie with a throat wound after surgery for thyroid cancer at our local hospital. Sister Marie told me about it and today brings her to me.

Rufina stands silently with her husband, Vicente. They've come on the jitney from their village. Rufina keeps her hands entwined and her face down. At the base of her throat, just above her shawl, is the clean dressing Marie has applied, but there is still some slight oozing. "I've been treating her," Sister Marie says, "and I agreed when the doctor in Puno recommended surgery, but now she needs care that they can't give. My postulants are just now due for their next stage of vows. I'd take her to Arequipa where she'd get better care, but I can't leave here now."

Sister Marie's face is drawn tight. It is so unlike her who I look up to for her ability to calmly manage whatever comes along with innate assurance. Her appearance seems effortless and impressive too. Her thick, honey blonde hair, which I guess doesn't get much fussing beyond washing and perfunctory morning brushes, sets off her fresh looks. She, like Sister Francie, is invariably dressed in jeans and a warm flannel shirt.

"I'll take her, Marie," I say, breathing deep. It has to be done. "I'll give you the charts of the patients I'm seeing so you can cover for me."

Marie sighs in relief. She translates to Rufina in Aymara, and the young mother gives a timid smile. It's settled. I'll take Rufina and her husband to Arequipa for improved care.

There are a couple of important things to resolve before we start out on our trip. Vicente and Rufino tell me their neighbors will take in their children, so that has been dealt with. But Vicente says if he doesn't vote in the current presidential election, he'll have to pay a fine.

President Fugimori is in exile from office. Alejandro Toledo is running, poised to become the first indigenous president. For Vicente, like all *campesinos*, subsistence farmers, any fine is a burden. I've witnessed whitewash splashed over another patient's house by local officials for noncompliance in elections.

So, Vicente and I go into Puno right then, so he can get an official vote waiver for a medical excuse. Rufina agrees to stay with Sister Marie.

On a side street in Puno, Vicente and I approach a man on a stool sitting at a high desk with a manual typewriter. Vicente hands over his identity papers, and the man slowly types a long, explanatory note for Vicente to show to his local officials. Back in Camacani, after the jeep is put away in the nuns' yard, I make ham sandwiches for the couple. They look back and forth at each

A Surprise

other at this strange food but seem to enjoy it. I ask them to come back the next day, after they've turned in the waiver and have double-checked on the arrangement for their five children. Their youngest is about two years old. They also have two early grade school kids, and the oldest are two girls in their teens. They agree to stay overnight at my place when they come back before our journey so we can catch an early bus.

When they arrive the next afternoon, I serve them chicken soup with the ever-faithful bread triangles. This is more familiar food for them, but the addition of chicken to the potato broth is something typically reserved for weddings or festivals. Fairly early in the evening, I lead them to the big double bed in the clinic.

Once they're settled, I go outside for a few quiet minutes. The sky in the Andes, far from city lights, is ablaze with hundreds of stars. I love seeing the Southern Cross in my upside-down world where December is the height of summer. I go in peace to my small bedroom and prepare for tomorrow's journey.

As I rouse them for breakfast the next morning, I see they have slept in their clothes.

Rufina is in layers of thick, full skirts, with a warm shawl over several sweaters. Her derby hat sits on the clinic desk. The completion of her classic look is her long, thick braid, reaching almost to her waist. Vicente has on thick trousers and a heavy jacket. I serve them oatmeal with almonds and raisins. Vicente, the more communicative of the two, is quick to say, "*¡Gracias Hermana!*" and tells me how good everything is.

Rufina, worried and scared and with little Spanish, impresses me as more somber and stoic, more typical of the majority of the people in the Aymara culture.

Right after we eat, we head over to Sister Francie's to get the jeep. It's too early for the nuns to be about. Just one sister is letting the dog out. She waves and signals she'll shut the big gate after me. Then we enjoy the ride along Lake Titicaca which sparkles with light as we pass.

I park inside the Maryknoll fathers' compound and let the fathers know. The jeep will be safe behind the locked iron gates no matter how long our trip. We walk the few blocks to the bus station, stopping at Rufina's brother's workplace. He's a *molinero*, a grain grinder, who works at a little shop in town.

We want to make sure he knows their five children are in the care of neighbors, and that he will stop in and check on them while Vicente and Rufina are gone. He is tall and could walk down a New York street without attracting notice, he is that modern in dress and appearance. He listens closely, rubbing his hands on his powdery apron, and assures his sister and brother-in-law that he will look in on the children.

The three of us then bustle off to the terminal. I am anxious to find the right bus in the large, dusty parking lot full of buses. Amid the smell of diesel fuel and honking horns, the drivers call out their destinations, "Lima! Juliaca! Arequipa!

Jumbled lines of passengers form around the bus doors. I search anxiously for a bathroom to use before we board as it could be hours before a stop. I make sure they each have the ten centavos required for toilet paper. If the bus does stop, it is usually for a few seriously uninviting outhouses. Most passengers just walk further back off the highway and find bushes for cover.

Chapter 18
A Trip to Arequipa

FINALLY ON THE BUS, Rufina and Vicente sit directly in front of me. It's hot, no fresh air at all, hard to breathe. Most of the windows are stuck shut. Mine is stuck open a two-inch crack. I'm on the inside and a large, silent man is close beside me in the aisle seat. I'm just managing being squeezed into the airless interior when Rufina asks me to switch seats. I decline. I grovel in guilt, but I need to be realistic. I'm the guiding force here.

Outside, a man has fallen to the pavement. People are gathered around him. Rufina gives me a searching look. I don't even consider getting off and offering CPR. I'm at my limit. At this moment the bus pulls out with a roar. I sink back in my seat for the five-hour ride to Arequipa.

At the Arequipa bus station, I help Vicente and Rufina off with their satchels, but when I go back for mine it's gone. My own satchel had in it a cherished black alpaca sweater, worn almost daily, and a red felt blanket my daughter had secretly slipped into my luggage after my last leave. It was doubly comforting to me and doubly disappointing.

I get the couple settled in at the bus terminal restaurant with soup and bread, and I cross the road to the off-duty bus yard, but to no avail. The guy in charge shows me the empty racks of our bus. I walk back, talking myself down from disappointment, reminding myself that it is Rufina, a mother of five with a botched surgery, who has the real pain. I join them for soup.

Now we need to find a place to stay. One of the Maryknoll sisters gave me the name and address of a *Señora* Regina, a retired hospital social worker here in Arequipa. The *señora* sent word she'd be happy to help. I need to find the boardinghouse she recommended.

I get us a taxi. We're in the outlying streets of Arequipa, not the downtown I've previously enjoyed with Lexi that has buildings of several stories and elegant shops.

The taxi stops in front of a sizable concrete house surrounded by a high wall. The lady of the house greets us at the front door, shielding her eyes from the bright sun, she smiles and nods.

"*Señora* Lucy, here to see *Señora* Regina? My name is Mercedes."

Mercedes ushers us inside through a cool corridor to a big courtyard out back. Ducking under a clothesline filled with clothes, she opens a door to a room for Vicente and Rufina. Just past a big white porcelain sink and up a few concrete steps is my room.

My room has a small patio outside with a waist-high concrete wall. I check back on Vicente and Rufina and bring them up to my room, so they'll know I'm right nearby.

That evening, I see how handy the patio will be. We walk around the corner and buy empanadas, fruit, cookies, and water and now sit at a little table up here for dinner. I light the candles I brought and set them on the patio wall. So far, so good. I begin to relax.

A Trip to Arequipa

The next day we taxi into the city to the hospital. We enter a large, very crowded concrete yard. The way it works, I learn by asking people in line, is that you start in a general long line then get to a window, where you are guided to the line specific to your problem. After snaking through that line, like at an airport, you make it to the window, where a nurse triages your case and guides you to a line to wait to see your proper doctor.

The first two days we're done by early afternoon. All of us are too tired to wait in another line, so we explore Arequipa a little. I always bring almonds with me, something I buy for myself every week at the big open market in Puno. They tide us over the long hours in line before we bring food back to our little patio in the evenings.

About the almonds, Vicente says, "*Estos matan el hambre muy bien, sí, hermana?*" "These kill the hunger good, right, Sister?"

As we're getting ready to go to the hospital the third day, I discover that *Señora* Regina has left a note inviting me to dinner this evening. She writes an address. I sit a few minutes on my patio, thinking. I'm torn between getting help from her local hospital knowledge and going along and maybe insulting my indigenous patient and her husband.

In the end, I buy Rufina and Vicente dinner when we return that evening, set up the candles for them, and explain I'll go talk to the *señora* and maybe it will help us.

It's a substantial house only a few blocks away on a quiet street, no traffic. I knock on the carved wooden door, a little nervous. We'll be speaking in Spanish. A young Indian woman answers, and I follow her soft tread to the living room where the *señora*, dressed in a dark skirt and white blouse, stands to greet me. She has high cheekbones and a crown of dark hair. She's wearing pearls. I'm glad I washed and ironed my best blouse in our courtyard the day before.

At dinner, the *señora* sweeps her hand toward the dining room furniture - big, dark mahogany pieces.

"We were fortunate to be able to save our furniture when they forced us out of our hacienda."

I know a little of what Regina is talking about. She brings it alive for me. From reading, I know that something called the Agrarian Reform Decree, supported by urban leftists in the '60s, resulted in widespread land distribution and the seizing of haciendas. Within decades the traditional Andean haciendas were no longer in the hands of the powerful oligarchy. I imagine Regina's family moving to Arequipa at that time, a total change of their lives and a great loss.

We don't dwell on that. She tells me the name of the doctor she most recommends at the hospital and gives a detailed orientation about how the hospital works. I tell her about Rufina's condition. It turns out to be a relaxing and cordial evening.

I walk home through the quiet streets, glad I went. I bring some dessert to Rufina and Vicente that Regina sent home with me. The three of us sit eating, watching our little patio candles, enjoying the cool night air.

The following day, when we finish waiting at the hospital by midafternoon, we walk and discover a little park. We sit on benches overlooking the green lawn, watching people pass.

"*Mira, Hermana,*" says Vicente, "*las palomas están comiendan.*" "Look, Sister, the pigeons are eating."

A Trip to Arequipa

Even Rufina chimes in, "*Sí las palomas están comiendan.*"

This is day four. I feel like I have run out of stick-to-it-tiveness. I buy them ice cream cones from a passing cart and say I have to do something and will be back very soon. They agree to stay *right there*. I walk quickly past the modern storefronts, relishing the sophisticated city atmosphere of downtown Arequipa, and head straight for a cybercafé I had visited on a previous trip with Lexi. It's lovely and smells good inside. I go up the stairs with a café con leche to where I remember there is a lone computer in a balcony corner, overlooking the downstairs. I pound out emails to Lexi and Mary Kate, who I miss so sorely at this moment. I am thrilled to hear back from both of them immediately. We wind up laughing together at my becoming so dramatically overwhelmed. Feeling 100 percent better, I hurry back to the park and greet Rufina and Vicente with smiles.

Finally, after one more day, we are with a doctor, who is listening closely to my succinct telling (thanks to my physician assistant training) of Rufina's story. He inspects her surgical site, looks up at me, and says, "Honey, you've got to take her to Lima. She needs the thyroid irradiated. That can only be done in Lima."

I feel relief and fatigue. Glad for a clear answer and resistant to the prospect of a longer journey. Nevertheless, the next day, I herd us back to the bus station, buy our tickets, and we are headed to Lima. We all have comfortable seats and plenty of fresh air in the much nicer bus.

When we arrive, I plow us past the throng of gesturing taxi drivers calling, "¡*Señora, señora!*" to a quieter street corner, where I can negotiate a better fare to take us to Miraflores, the gracious residential part of Lima where the Maryknoll House is located.

Vicente and Rufina's eyes are wide as we pass streets of shops and fast-moving cars. They crane out the window, pointing out the flashing lights of the downtown casinos to each other. They look in amazement at the huge cigarette advertisement billboard with the cowboy blowing smoke, then look at me, then burst out laughing. They've never seen the like!

At the Maryknoll House, where Lexi and I had orientation with Derek two years before, we are greeted by my friend, Father Stephen. I know him from his frequent visits to Puno, sharing community meals and evening conversations with him. He is also a singer with the Maryknoll choir up in New York, so we share that interest. He lives in the Lima House and is based here. He invites us to stay as long as we need, no charge, including meals. What a lovely respite! We settle in and begin spending our days waiting in line at the hospital in downtown Lima, *Instituto de Enfermedades Neoplastico*, Institute of Neoplastic Diseases.

Steve, who is happy for a companion, asks me to join him for his evening walks around a nearby olive grove full of gnarled, ancient trees and the remains of an old manual olive press. We talk books, movies, life. He mentions a mutual friend of ours, who works at the Puno House, who had mistaken his friendship for romance.

I say very clearly, because I cherish his friendship and don't want to lose it, "I think of you as a dedicated priest. I remember going with you to visit the poorest parishes. You attend all the baptisms and weddings of the people, giving up your Sundays. You are the real article."

The real article is my highest compliment. I've said it about honest doctors dedicated to their patients, true healers.

A Trip to Arequipa

After that conversation, we continue our walks and Scrabble games with no confusion about who we are to each other. Steve has been diagnosed with Burkitt's lymphoma, a blood cancer. Maryknoll is providing the best of care. He flew up to Sloan Kettering for a bone marrow transplant. Back in Lima now, he is doing well, eating a vegetarian diet and walking on a regular basis. I revere him and appreciate his stories and rollicking sense of humor.

The hospital in Lima is a whole different world from Arequipa. There are the long lines, but we are waiting inside a large, sunny lobby with benches and nearby restrooms. Various departments are clearly marked on doors. In two days, Rufina is scheduled for the procedure.

Today we're here for it. The nurse is saying I can't go in with Rufina to be prepped. I don't take no for an answer.

"Rufina has very little Spanish, and she's already overwhelmed being in a big modern hospital. I can translate and support her," I say, walking forward with Rufina.

In the prep room, the young nurse applies a razor to Rufina's hairline. I want to say that shaving the skin increases the chance of infection by opening micro cuts in the skin, but I keep my mouth shut. Until she holds the scissors at Rufina's braid.

I stop her. "That's not necessary. We can put a surgical cap on her." We are done. Rufina goes off to the procedure, braid intact.

By the end of the afternoon, I collect Rufina to get us home to the Maryknoll House.

The doctor explains to me that the irradiation dose that Rufina has received could damage the thyroid of anyone in close proximity to her for several days. She needs to be isolated.

In the taxi I have her sit in back and I sit in front, holding the thick book I've been reading in front of my neck. The taxi driver has a leather jacket with a thick collar he turns up. She looks hurt and confused and even more so when I place her in a separate room at the house and hand in her meals for the next couple of days. I try to explain as I bring her meals, but I don't think she understands.

Finally, we are ready to travel back to Puno. I sit close to Rufina on the bus, and she seems reassured. But when she comes soon afterward for a follow-up visit with me, she's quiet and seems depressed.

Only as I discuss it with Sister Marie, who asks me about the dosage of her thyroid medication, do I realize in the flurry of getting them back home that I haven't ordered thyroid replacement meds for her now nonfunctioning but cancer-free thyroid. I get her established on the medicine that same day, but Rufina, living far out in an isolated community, still seems sad. I look into moving them near me in Camacani, but I have no means to offer them support beyond medicine. My heart hurts for her. She's well now, but struggling with a lonely, hard life.

Today, I'm visiting her out in their community. We walk to the school and walk back to their home with her two young teen daughters in school uniforms. They fuss over their mother and make her giggle. In this moment she seems happy. I'm reassured to see her laugh and enjoy them. Hopefully that will be enough.

Chapter 19
Experienced With a Lot to Learn

DURING THIS TIME without Lexi and Mary Kate, I plan one more trip to Lima to get needed care for local patients. This trip also involves patients of Sister Marie's and both young women have become frequent visitors to my house while we work out our trip.

In my yard hanging wash, they teach me the words for clothespins, *pinzas de la ropa*, and wrinkles, *arrugas*. They laugh at my strange ways: my many books, my refrigerator, my awkward Spanish. Today we're having tea and cookies in the kitchen. They like the nice light - wood furniture made by my neighbor, Rene, and the view from the window of people passing on the path below.

Angelica lives in the next community. Maria Elena lives further out. They are the same age, about eighteen or nineteen. They've known each other from church and school groups. Angelica has a recurring infection in one of her eyes. I come close to losing my temper with the doctor who is treating her with an endless series of eye drops. He hasn't established the cause. Her vision is becoming impaired. He's not the real article. But even as I let out a little frustration at him, I know it's a dumb move. I need all the good doctor connections I can get.

Maria Elena is diabetic. Sister Marie has kept her supplied with medication, but her teeth are rotting and deformed and it's changing her life. She hides her smile behind her cupped hand; she's becoming shy and passive.

I'm staying close to both girls until we can work out getting us to Lima. In the meantime, cases in my own clinic are keeping me busy. A new mother comes with a painful, swollen breast, which is interfering with nursing her newborn. I show her how to do hot soaks with new diapers, emphasizing they must be kept washed and spotlessly clean as she reuses them. I give her antibiotic pills and a pack of diapers.

A few days later I'm driving out to her remote village to check on her. I park on the outskirts, wary of a dog barking at me from the perimeter. A man approaches, quieting the dog.

"Are you the one who helped my daughter?"

"Yes." I hold up my medical bag. "I've come to see her, see if she's good now."

A tall man with a long stride, his dark jacket swinging, he walks me back along a dried mud ridge that borders a narrow canal. We come to a group of simple houses.

I poke my head inside at his gesture of invitation and see the young mother. She's not in pain, looking well, and holding her beautiful baby boy. Yes, she has taken the pills and done the hot soaks, and the pain and swelling are gone. We are all smiling.

The father escorts me back to the jeep. I feel a bloom of happiness in my chest, *how good to get something right.*

On a typical day, walking down my path, medical bag in hand, going the long way round to the sisters' yard for the Land Rover, my neighbor Rene asks, "*¿Dónde va, Hermana?*" "Where are you going, Sister?"

"*Un paciente.*" "A patient." "*¿Quien?*" "Who?"

"*Es privado, como caundo visito tu.*" "It's private, like when I visit you."

They make me laugh sometimes. In some ways they are like children, open and frank, not above being a little conniving. But in many ways, they possess an ancient wisdom that has them surviving in an almost no-money economy: houses of dried mud, farm implements of tree limbs and precious purchased blades, tea from bushes, potatoes and quinoa from their fields.

For cash they count on selling a cow or sheep if need be. Rene makes furniture to sell, accompanying his wife, Patricia, on the jitney if there is too much for her to carry. The women knit shawls and socks and weave beautifully colored fabric.

Today I have a visit from Silva's wife, Flora. She visits now and then since I took her husband to the hospital, where X-rays showed arthritis. She tells me he continues to do much better. He is more active and doing the stretching exercises I gave him. Flora takes the opportunity to sell me a few hand-knitted finger puppets that the women sell everywhere, even wagging them on their fingers through restaurant windows to make a sale.

As we sit together at the clinic desk, I start walking the Red Riding Hood puppet like she's going through the woods. Flora starts stalking behind with the Wolf. Then Red Riding Hood gets to her grandmother's house and Flora covers the wolf with the end of her shawl.

"*¡Abuela, que gran ojos tiene!*" "Grandmom, what big eyes you have!"

"*Sí, mi dulce.*" "Yes, my sweet." We both start laughing at ourselves and the happiness of connecting. And Silva is flourishing.

The day arrives and Maria Elena, Angelica, and I are at the bus terminal with our tickets for Lima. It's about a twenty-hour trip, so we'll travel through the night. This time, having learned my lesson, I chose the best bus I could find with seats that recline and a bathroom on board. They are young, thrilled to be going to the big city. We have appointments in the city and arrive a day ahead so the girls can enjoy Lima. I take them to a department store that has an escalator. Up we go.

"Let's do it again!" they say. We go up and down several times, with them waving and laughing at themselves in the mirrored side walls.

We walk to the Pacific and head for the pocket park, high above the ocean, with the colorful mosaics embedded in the boulders along the path.

Back at the Maryknoll House, they stick by me in the dinner line. The cooks have made a favorite dessert, rice pudding from scratch. Actually, everything here is cooked from scratch.

The Maryknoll fathers greet the girls like visiting princesses.

The first appointment next morning is Angelica's. We all go together in a taxi. As we drive downtown, I'm becoming wary of the driver. He's acting spacey, asking us again and again where we're going. As soon as I recognize the hospital neighborhood from an exploratory visit, I say, "We'll get out here."

We walk the rest of the few blocks, a safer bet, and enter the hospital. We search out our doctor for the appointment. The building is modern and organized. After a few turns in the hallways, with polite people guiding us, we're soon in the doctor's exam room. Maria Elena and I watch as he looks with his optical equipment directly into Angelica's eye.

Experienced With a Lot to Learn

I'm a bit taken aback by the diagnosis and treatment plan. Herpes infection of the right eye, requiring removal of the affected cornea. The doctor lays out the plan. He gives me a list of what I will need to purchase at the pharmacy. They will procure the cornea. I'm given a price for that. This is standard procedure in Peru. I have planned and saved for this. I give the go-ahead and schedule.

The next day, Maria Elena and I walk over to consult a local dentist recommended by the Lima fathers. I had hoped to be able to afford dental transplants, but the cost, I learn, as the dentist discusses her case, is thousands of dollars. Maria Elena and I walk home past the beautiful houses and palm trees of this upscale neighborhood, talking about whether or not she wants to consider false teeth, the second option, which can be done in stages over several weeks. Maria Elena wants to do it. I talk about the drawbacks of false teeth, the pain of the procedure, and that it can't be undone, but she is clear. "I want to do it."

I can stay and can afford this plan, so we set Maria Elena's dental appointments.

For the next few days, I'm taxiing back and forth to visit Angelica, who's recuperating from surgery tucked in her hospital bed. Finally, the eye patch is removed, and she is seeing well with no signs of infection. I'll bring her home tomorrow.

While in the foyer this morning waiting for my ride, Steve joins me. "I'd like to go with you to bring Angelica home."

"Oh! That would be great!" I see he has flowers for her. "She will be so pleased and honored that you came!"

And she is exactly that to see him there, and also bubbling over to be released, thrilled that her eye is clear and that she is seeing "*perfectamente!*"

She hugs us both and thanks Steve for the flowers. "¡Gracias, muchisimus gracias!" Padre Stephen!"

She then looks directly at me, who's been teaching her some English, and says, "Thank you, *Hermana*."

We ride home quietly, each seemingly content, counting our blessings. Then Steve says out of the blue, "Do you know how the devil gets good people?"

He's talking English to me. Angelica is happily absorbed, looking out the window. I turn to him, and he continues.

"Because, you know, good people are not going to start robbing banks or killing people. What the devil does is turn them on themselves. Fills them with self-doubt and self- criticism."

I get it.

We ride home, the three of us in the taxi, me with my arms wrapped around a bundle of Angelica's clothes while she is clutching her flowers and putting her face into them occasionally, smelling them deeply.

I think, *is Steve saying that specifically to me?*

He is, I realize. And I conclude that he has seen me fully, the real me. This is his gift to me!

What I don't know at this moment in the taxi riding through Lima is that it will send me on a lifelong journey of healing and self-acceptance.

Chapter 20

The Next Step

BACK IN PUNO, with the girls settled, I ponder, *what next?* The end date of my three-year commitment is coming in a couple of months. Over the next few weeks, I keep mulling it over.

And I have a wonderful distraction. Jack and Jane, my son and his wife, come to visit.

We explore it all: Lima, Arequipa, my village home, and finally Machu Picchu. It's my first visit there too.

The central plaza is crowded. We learn to fend off with a finger wag the many merchants offering local goods. Then we check our tickets and realize we need to rush to catch the train up to Machu Picchu. As we clamber on board the conductor says, "This is the last train up today to Machu Picchu!" Up at the site the kids want to scamper up one more level of the ancient site. I wait, sitting on the edge of a cliff overlooking the tops of mountains. I am in awe, feeling the sacredness of Machu Picchu that I've read about.

I feel a clearness and a peace. I am so alive and so grateful.

After the kids depart, I do decide to at least explore Oaxaca, Mexico, where there is a Maryknoll couple I like and admire and a small hospital with a good reputation where I could gain medical knowledge from the doctors and nurses and be part of a community. I think an extended visit there would help me decide whether or not to commit to Maryknoll for another three years, and I begin making plans for it.

I'm soon on my way. The easy part of the journey to Oaxaca is the plane ride, but once we land, I begin to get overwhelmed trying to locate a bus to take me to the house of the missioners where I'm invited to stay for the week. Partly, it's operating in a language other than my own.

Partly it's me, prone to getting anxious when caught up in the details of accomplishing almost anything.

In Oaxaca's crowded, more modern bus station, I finally find the right ticket window.

I'm frantically searching through my bulky bag, my purse, my pockets for my passport.

At wit's end, I throw my journal and pen to the floor, ready to crumple there in tears myself. I pull it together and find my passport and the right currency and get my ticket and board the bus. I have the address in my hand as I board, and the driver reassures me that I am on the right bus, and he will alert me when my stop is nearby.

Much of the rest of the week is a blur. The receiving couple couldn't be kinder or more welcoming. I visit the various workplaces of all the missioners stationed there. Most importantly, I visit the hospital where I would be working. The hospital staff has arranged to give me a thorough tour, and afterward we gather in the conference room.

I am impressed with the site and the staff. It's a modern two-story building with various offices for different specialties surrounding a large patio. These offices serve outpatients, but there also is a four-bed impatient section used for surgeries.

The Next Step

The staff wants to know about my previous physician assistant experience, and I want to know details about their daily work. I know it would be a wonderful learning experience, and it's appealing as a next three-year commitment.

I'm honest with the staff that after working only three years at an outpatient practice in the US, and establishing a simple clinic in Peru, I'd be looking to learn from them. They seem okay with that. And I'd be happy to teach English. I'd surely be fluent in Spanish working there. I feel encouraged and happy.

I am also very happy to reverse my journey and wend my way back to my simple home in the mountains, finally taking the jitney from the airport to the Center House in Puno and driving the jeep home. The next morning, I'm sitting at the kitchen table, sipping coffee, looking over my landlady's quinoa field and the simple footpath below. A few folks are walking by switching a donkey. Below that is the large, paved road where the buses and jitneys run, and just past it, a few glints of light sparkling from Lake Titicaca.

I'm writing in my journal, thinking of Oaxaca, thinking of what an amazing life path that would be, with more medical training, more Spanish fluency, and moving deeper into the simple, richly rewarding spiritual life of a missioner.

And then, sipping coffee and writing, I draw myself up short. I'm not thinking of Oaxaca! To my surprise, I'm daydreaming about Lewes, Delaware. I'm picturing a life there. I had visited the quaint town several times from my home in Palmyra, New Jersey, about a two - hour ride away. My old high school friend Cathy- ("I have no opinion about that.") - and her husband, Malachi, live there. On my visit to Lewes during a yearly home trip, she said I could easily get a medical job there as a community near her has a large Latina population. And I loved the old town, minutes from the ocean.

I am a little bemused at this unexpected turn, but somehow, I don't feel torn. I feel, to my surprise, clear and convicted. In spite of all its rational advantages, Oaxaca is fading. My energy is going toward a new home, one in the small town near the ocean, and most importantly, where I will be in the same country as my children.

In the two months until the end of my commitment in Peru, I work the clinic as usual. I have an important focus with a family whose three-year-old boy, Kim, has lost his hearing after a severe ear infection. Likely he did not receive the antibiotics he needed from the thin-stretched Puno hospital. I find him hearing aids, traveling to a pharmacy across the border in Bolivia, but over the next few weeks I see the father and mother are struggling to use them consistently.

I begin working with a US hospital to get him there for a cochlear transplant, but it is a long process. His parents need visas. We make trips back and forth to Puno to obtain them, but I can see they are uneasy about it and reluctant. It is a huge leap for them, and eventually negotiations break down with the sponsoring group and the surgeon. I leave it with the parents that they will persevere with the hearing aids.

Then, I have something else to deal with. My daughter alerts me that the renters in my house in New Jersey have stopped paying the rent. It's difficult to work this out by email. I am pretty overwhelmed, and one evening at the Center House I pour out my anxiety to Sister Pat. She takes in my story patiently. It turns

The Next Step

out that by the time the bank alerted my daughter, the mortgage was two months behind. This is my home base, my wonderful, beautiful house, and no matter what I decide about my future, this is my security. I feel panicky.

Sister Pat, in her calm, reassuring fashion, says, "This hasn't unfolded yet," and her thoughts and manner center me. I go into action. I ask my daughter to pay the mortgage. She does, no problem. Then I get in touch with Maryknoll. I need to leave a few weeks ahead of the end of my contract. They understand. I wrap up everything with my patients, talking it over in detail with Sister Marie.

Rene, my neighbor, who made all my furniture, now helps me hire a truck to pack it up and put it in storage in Father Bob's large seminary storeroom. We all make the half-hour trip along the big highway to Juli, Rene's father and his boys coming along.

I follow in the Jeep, rented from Father Bob these three years, to return it to him. I leave the rock and large nail on the front seat with a thank you note and a cartoon drawing of Lexi and me starting the car with these tools.

I say goodbye to everybody: my neighbors, the sisters, especially our dear Sister Francie. Lexi wrote with an idea to make a Sister Francie doll for a goodbye/thank you present. I concoct a jeans-clad, flannel- shirted doll with big angel wings sticking out the back. Of course she loves it, and we laugh and hug. I think she is disappointed to lose me; my medical skills and an extra pair of hands are always needed. I think she hoped I had made a lifetime commitment. She had poured a lot of work and time into helping me get established.

But soon I'm on my way, flying over the yellow and green patchwork fields of Peru, half heartsore. I remember one set of visitors to my little dwelling saying, "You've found heaven."

And I am clear. I fly first to Maryknoll to muster out: sign paperwork and have a final health check. That evening when I settle into my familiar and welcoming room in the old convent, I am pinching myself. I did it! All I have to do for the next few days is walk back and forth up the hill, in upstate New York's pleasant summer weather, to the clinic in the fathers' gracious building for routine doctor visits.

I also fit in a visit to Lexi that week, in Manhattan, and as fate would have it, MaryKate is visiting the city too with her parents. The three of us - one good missioner - go to see Steve, now at Maryknoll in hospice care. Sitting at a table with us, thinner than ever, he loves our gift, a book of Shakespeare's sonnets. We reminisce, laughing over our shared experiences of Peru. He tells us wonderful stories of his mother, that when she became a new widow, the mother of five, sitting them around their kitchen table, she said, "We have to make it together now."

Back at Maryknoll, I am packing my bag to leave the next day when somebody knocks on my door and says I have a telephone call from one of the fathers, Father Gorky. When I pick it up downstairs in the office, he asks if I could come up to the fathers' house and meet with him.

I know Joe Gorky from Maryknoll's language school, where Lexi and I and our class started our mission tour in Cochabamba, Bolivia. At that time, he asked me to have a talk with one of the woman missioners in our class who was having angry outbursts. I had witnessed one. I remember being flattered that Father Joe saw me as sensible and stable, good for the task. It was who I aspired to be but doubted deep down that I was.

Nonetheless, I think the missioner and I had a useful talk. She had lost a grandchild under tragic circumstances, a fire. I remember her saying, "If I give in to depression, I fear I'll never come out of it. If I stay angry, I'm okay."

It seemed to help her to own what was going on.

But now, sitting in Joe's office, he presents me with a task of a whole different magnitude.

Would I come to work with him in Guatemala as my next three-year commitment? He runs a shelter for homeless young men there, street kids who are now young adults. I could picture myself cooking, organizing, counseling. I feel honored. I say I'll give it serious thought and will let him know soon. I walk back down the hill in a daze.

The next morning, stuffing the last few things into my suitcase, I look around my room, remembering how I loved moving in there with only my best and needed stuff, all displayed on the open shelves that cover one wall. Paring down my life to simplicity and purpose has been a sheer joy. I don't want to change that no matter how I move forward.

I'll be catching the train to Philadelphia from the nearby Ossining station. From there I'll take the speed line to Camden, New Jersey. Then a quick ride on what I call the Tooterville Trolly, practically to the doorstep of my house in Palmyra. That last leg from Philadelphia had been my daily trip to the Hahnemann School of Allied Medicine, when I trained as a physician assistant.

Father Joe's offer has me feeling like someone in a movie. Not a heroic figure, but myself in a new light, a deep core of serenity and self-acceptance along with my usual anxiety. I am thrilled and scared, grateful and overwhelmed, and now confused.

I was on a short mission to Guatemala not far from where Father Joe is proposing I would work. I loved it all: beautiful, rolling green countryside, the warm, expressive people. It takes me a long time to fall asleep. Scenes of my role as a house mother/counselor/experienced missioner play in my head.

The longest part of the next day's journey is soothing. I love train rides, effortlessly rocking along in a smooth rhythm, moving toward my destination with no effort on my part, without the back-burner anxiety I feel when traveling high in the clouds in an airplane.

I'm mulling over Father Joe's proposal, watching the back of houses, smiling as we pass the Hudson River, remembering so many delightful walks there during training.

And somehow, I know.

I want to live in the same country as my grown children. I don't want to be just a colorful character in their stories.

"What does your mother do?"

"Oh, she's a medical missioner up in the Andes Mountains in Peru."

I want a life intertwined with theirs. Day-to-day stuff, holidays, visits.

I start sketching out a letter to Father Joe on the train. "Thank you. Sorely tempting, but no."

When I get home, I have a few more mountains to climb. My son pays the one more missed mortgage payment. I soon pay back both kids and start clearing out my junked-up house.

The Next Step

The renters left beds, table, and chairs along with broken windows and scratched-up doors. With the help of my dear friend Dolores, who had earlier cautioned me against the whole PA/mission venture, we tackle it. We are laughing as she heaves a twin mattress down the stairs. On a break we sit on the floor, backs against the wall, eating yogurt she's brought with her.

For a short time, I live in my empty house with only an air mattress, a big carton for a table, and a new coffee mug. Very Zen-like. I love it. I am amazed at how big the cars are-SUVs, they call them. In a grocery store I turn to answer the woman behind me who has talked to me— or so I think—but she is talking on her cell phone, a new experience for me. I am a little shaky.

I visit another lifelong friend, Dori in Philadelphia, who I met way back in our ER days evaluating patients for mental health commitment. When I bring my own comfortable blanket with me to stay over at their house, she is totally kind and accepting. I am coming home to some wonderful friends.

Cynthia, another dear friend, part of the single-again group of women who often went over the bridge to the cinema arts movie in Philadelphia, offers to help clean up my house. Funny thing is, Cynthia, a kind, ego-free woman —we worked together as clinical social workers—has probably never cleaned in her life. She valiantly attempts a few kitchen cabinets, then laughing says, "I'm no good at this!" Only after she has gone, do I discover she has left me a check.

I soon find a physician assistant job in Lewes, Delaware, rent a house, get my furniture out of storage and move in. Mary Beth and Johanna from the Catholic Worker clinic arrange for their young premed students to paint the rooms in my New Jersey house, making it easier to rent again.

And *I am experiencing me*, unheroic, real, more centered and more joyful than I had ever known.

After about a year in Lewes, my daughter and her husband spend a weekend with me back at the New Jersey house when we put it on the market. Rod fixes holes in the wall, Trish scrubs kitchen cabinets, and I do the floors with a rental scrubber. My son Jack and his wife Jane, who live in Colorado, soon come to visit in Lewes—all of them together—in my rented house five minutes from the ocean. The joint rocks. The girls keep the towels washed and restocked in the one bathroom. We rent bikes and play bocce ball in the nearby park.

As I settle into the routine of my PA job, I find a wonderful church and weekly meditation group. The memory of that ride home from the hospital in Lima with Steve often comes back to me. On that ride home from the hospital in Lima, Steve said, "You know how the devil brings down good people?" I remembered his answer, "He turns them on themselves."

I realized the incalculable value of being truly seen by one person and the paltry value of being misjudged by myriads of others—and yourself. Steve died a few weeks after our New York visit.

I loved my time in mission. I cherish my connection with Maryknoll. I admire people who do make a lifetime commitment to mission. Like Coraliss, whose dinners nobody in our training group ever missed, and Russ, "Can you *do* that?!" Both are still working in mission sites.

Lexi lives in Sweden with her husband, who reconnected with her after she returned.

The Next Step

They met in his country many years ago. Mary Kate is also happily married to a woman with children. She works in real estate. We remain in good touch.

I found peace and found my lifelong calling, my family. And along the way, I found me. It took a lot of my lifetime, but I caught the last train.

About the Author

HANNAH HANNON was a long-time clinical social worker in individual and family therapy before training as a physician assistant. With new medical skills practiced in the U.S., Hannah undertook a three-year mission to the Aymara people in the Andes Mountains of Peru.

She's been writing all her life, starting with filling blank pages of newspapers on a gift typewriter from an uncle returning from WWII. She is in several writing groups.

Hannah lives in Delaware, a ferry ride away from two of her kids in New Jersey and a cross-country train ride to her two kids in Colorado. She currently works as a facilitator of a cancer support group.